Contents

Erna's story begins Behind the Green Door.

FOREWORD

A Family's story must be recorded in order for it to endure beyond two generations. (Erna's philosophy)

This conviction compelled me to write the de Burger Family Memoirs —for my children, my grandchildren, my great grandson, my siblings born in Canada as well as for my nieces and nephews.

I began to write these accounts in 2006 but life intervened and it is only now that I am ready to compile the events of my life into this book form.

Erna de Burger Fex

2021

*Special gratitude to my daughter Jacquie who was an immense help in polishing this book.

DEDICATED: to MY HUSBAND ALEX
And
OUR THREE BEAUTIFUL DAUGHTERS -
JACQUIE, MICHELLE, ALLISON

*You gave my life love and purpose –
And I thank you for those most precious gifts!*

Journey to my Past

IT WAS 2006 when I began to delve into the recesses of my mind to relive my past. Writing on's memoirs is interesting, pleasurable, and depending on the events discussed, can and does evoke strong feelings. These emotions range from euphoria to extreme sadness but are all welcome as memories come flooding back. It is my personal history and it is therefore important to me.

I have been asked very frequently, "How do you remember so many details?" The answer is quite simple really. As I begin to write it is as if a memory box opens and the happenings come flooding to the forefront on my mind. Suddenly I am transported back to my childhood in The Netherlands, to our sea voyage to Canada in 1951, meeting my husband Alex in 1959, our wedding, my children and grandchildren and great grandson. I visit again various homes where I have resided, revisit activities both enjoyable and not so much fun. Seeing myself picking blueberries in Creighton, standing before my first class at Creighton Mine Public School—fearful, yet proud, these bring back the sights, sounds and smells of those by-gone days.

The impetus for writing my memoirs began for me as an important legacy for my descendants. Family history must be written to endure. That has always been essential to me. An advertisement in Northern Life in 2006, offering a one-day course under the aegis of "Voice Print" spurred me on to begin writing my life stories. The course was taught by editor Vicki Gilhula. She began by saying, "Every person has a story." Immediately I realized that this was the type of writing I needed to do.

Consequently, when I discovered the Memoir Writing Group at Parkside Older Adults Centre and became acquainted with the members there, I knew I had found a home. Tuesday afternoon at one pm became a priority in my life.

Although we are from varying backgrounds and education, we share the common thread of wanting to record and share our life history. An unexpected wonderful result of this is been that we have become a support group for each other. We rejoice in the birth of a new grandchild and celebrate a special anniversary. Equally, we support each other through difficult times of life. Showing our caring has brought us close to each other. We have learned so much about each other's lives that long explanations are unnecessary.

My Family of Origin

My family of origin is the de Burger Family. The de Burger chronology of my father, Florent de Burger, is traced back to the early twentieth century. My grandfather, Johannes de Burger was born on November 28, 1880 in the Town of Clinge in the province of Zeeland, The Netherlands. He was a farmer. His wife, Julia Maria Willaert, was born October 29, 1887, also in Clinge. At the time of their marriage in 1906, Johannes was 26 and Julia was 23 years of age. Julia avoided being labelled a "spinster" in her community at that time. She tragically died of the Spanish Flu in 1919 leaving behind her husband and four young sons. My father (born in 1915) was the youngest, and was just four years old at this tender time in his life. As a widower, Johannes could not care for four little boys and work on the farm as well. Julia's family, the Willaerts, took in Florent and Bernard, the two youngest boys while the two oldest boys, Charles and Frans, remained on the farm with their father. The little boys lived there for a period of several years until Johannes married Appalonia Philomena Bruggeman. Johannes died in Hulst in 1946 of a kidney ailment at the age of 66. Florent and Bernard bonded with their Willaert cousins, a closeness which remained all of their lives. Whenever Florent visited The Netherlands, a visit with that caring family was a must.

Their stepmother Philomena Bruggeman de Burger was the only mother the brothers ever knew since they were too young to remember Julia. Philomena gave birth to a daughter, Maria, the first and only sister for the boys. They loved their mother and sister very much. I never heard my father or his brothers refer to them as stepmother or half-sister. I never knew the difference until I was 9 or 10 years old.

My mother is Alice Camilla van den Branden. Her parents were Joseph Petrus van den Branden and Emerentia de Block. My grandfather was born in 1886 in Vogelwaarde near Hulst. My grandmother was born in 1896 in Hulst. They married September 2, 1915.

Eight children were born of this union namely, Gustaaf, Alice, Louisa, Celina, Annie, Rachel and Corrie. An infant son, Emiel, died. Joseph's mother disowned him because his wife was of a lower class, and never spoke to him again. Such things were important in those days. When the family travelled to Hulst from the neighbouring St. Jansteen, she would turn her back while seated on her stoop as they passed by. She had no interest in her eight grandchildren. Emerentia died February 2, 1965 of hardening of the arteries in her brain. They had been married 49 1/2 years and plans were well underway for a grand celebration for their Golden Wedding Anniversary in September. My grandfather was devastated. He died May 25, 1977 at the venerable age of 92 . Just two of their children remain now in 2020, Corrie and Rachel. Rachel has dementia and seldom recognizes anyone.

My parents, Florent de Burger and Alice van den Branden, were married on February 15, 1941 in St. Jansteen, now part of Hulst. Alice was born in Hontenisse, near St. Jansteen on November 8, 1919. Florent was born Clinge on December 2, 1915. They met at a dance on Saturday a night in the village of Graauw, close to Hulst. They had 7 children, Erna (1941), Ronald (1942), Willy (1944), Frank (1948). All born in Holland. Marianne (1952), Liesje (1953), and Lillian (1960), were born in Canada. Now in 2020, just four of their children remain—Erna, Frank, Liesje and Lillian. Our parents operated a small fruit and vegetable store in Hulst at Langebellingstraat 6 close to the Market Square. With the birth of another son, Willy in 1944 they required more space and wanted a much larger store as well. The new store at Stationsweg 24 flourished and the family lived there until we immigrated to Canada. Another son Franky was born while we lived there, in 1948. They enjoyed their middle-class status. Many close extended family members and dear friends lived close by. Alice could afford, and needed a housekeeper, as she worked in the store 6 days weekly and had 4 young children. So, Lona came into our lives to take care of the children and do the housework. She made no secret that my brother Willy was her favourite.

We immigrated to Canada on October 2, 1951. Florent was 36 and Alice was 32 with four children under the age of ten, Erna, Ronald, Willy and Franky. We sailed across the ocean aboard the large immigrant ship De Volendam. It was a courageous undertaking, to leave the devastation of the post-WW11 Netherlands to find a better future for their children. The family's lives were changed dramatically in every way possible. Language, customs, family support, the birth of Marianne 1952 and her death in 1953, birth of Mary Alice (Liesje) six weeks later, accidental death of Willy 1960 at age 15, and the birth of Lillian 6 weeks later. No family support as they were too far away and even phone calls were an impossible expense. This made all of these events so much more painful.

The status of the family changed drastically from middle class to being poor. It was difficult for my parents to accept.

The family moved five times in the first two years ending with a stable period of living in Dogpatch between Creighton and Lively, for seven years. We lived there long enough to finally make Canadian friends. Florent worked deep underground in Creighton Mine. After my brother Willy was killed by a car while riding his bike on the road in front of the house in 1960, Florent and Alice moved to Whitefish where they operated a successful convenience store, like many hard-working immigrants do today. After Florent had several serious heart attacks he had to take a disability pension from Inco, the mining company. After just 12 years of service, his pension was small and the income from the store augmented the family's income. In 1969, the family relocated to Wallaceburg, a small friendly town in South Western Ontario where they again had a flourishing store until they retired in 1972. They enjoyed this lovely town of mostly Dutch immigrants and felt at home there immediately. They purchased a small pretty house nearby and lived there happily until their deaths. Alice died at age 76 after a long illness (non-alcoholic cirrhosis) in 1997. They had been married 56 years. Florent lived 10 years more until 2007. He died at the age of nearly 92 years, of heart disease. They are buried beside each other in Riverview Cemetery in Walllaceburg, as they had wished.

~ DE BURGER ~

SINCE 1697

De Burger is another synonym for the word humble. People who were described as De Burger never let the attention get to their heads, preferring instead to do good in the world without calling attention to themselves. Others found people with the last name De Burger to be a breath of fresh air.

Definition

de Burger Family Historical Documents

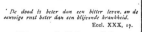

She was Florent's biological mother. She died when he was just 3 years old.

Julia Willaert de Burger

de Burger Family 1943

Back row: Charles, Maria, Florent

Front row: Bernard, Johannes & Philomena, Frans

HULST

THE SMALL CITY of Hulst in the province of Zeeland, in The Netherlands, is where I was born on June 7, 1941. It boasts itself as the "Most Flemish City in The Netherlands" and it is so because of its proximity to Belgium. The City of Hulst was incorporated in 1180. Hulst celebrated its' 800-year Anniversary in 1980. The Belgian city of Antwerp is just 30 minutes away and many Hulsternaars go there for shopping and entertainment.

Hulst is a walled city with three imposing stone entrances allowing entry to the centre of the old city. Huge berms called "De Wal" were constructed in 1620 for protection from invaders and are there yet today giving the city a medieval atmosphere even in this 21st century. Whenever I go to my birth place, a pleasurable walk on the footpaths on De Wal is a must. Strolling around the entire old city is peaceful and most interesting. Trees have been planted on de Wal making it a delightful walk. Surrounding de Wal is a circular moat which has swans, ducks and geese swimming in it. That was also built as additional protection for Hulst many years ago.

Hulst has many beautiful historic buildings and the most impressive of all is the Basilica, called Baseliek in Dutch. My three brothers and I were baptized in this remarkable Catholic Church and it was our parish until we immigrated to Canada in 1951. It's an enormous Gothic structure built in the 12th century and still in use today. I attend Mass there whenever I am in my hometown. Another notable building is the tall Windmill built in 1792 and also still operating today. It was most recently renovated in 1992. It is a functioning windmill with a certified miller making flour from grain provided by farmers in the area. Hulsternaars are justifiably proud of this. By making a reservation, tours are available and Alex and I had this privilege in 2007. The city hall called het Stadhuis, stands at the market place. It was constructed from 1528 – 1547 and is still in use today as well.

One day, I somehow escaped from the store and climbed up those high stairs when I was two years old. I rolled down its tall cement steps much faster that I had ascended. Thankfully I was not hurt – a surprise for sure. Civic weddings are held there and my sister Lillian, my brother Ron and I attended the lovely wedding of my cousin Hans Picavet and his beautiful bride Diana in 1985. Their beautiful wedding in the basilica followed that later in the afternoon.

Originally, Hulst was a port city with a harbour in the Middle Ages with access to the to the Schelde River, which leads to the North Sea. The ruins of this harbour have been uncovered recently and one can clearly envision it as it was. In 1795, Hulst lost its connection because a planned canal leading to the Schelde River was never built.

During WWII, Hulst was at the frontlines. We were liberated by Polish and Canadian soldiers in 1944. The tall steeple of the basilica was used as an observation post by the Nazis and thus had to be destroyed. A new steeple was added in 1957 in a modernistic style which does not suit the Gothic architecture of the church.

The centre of Hulst, as in many European towns and cities, is the market place. The cafes which are nearby offer perfect places to socialize no matter what the weather (heaters are used in winter). I really enjoy sitting there too and chatting with my aunts and cousins and we often have a beverage, coffee in the morning and something different in the afternoon or evening. The market place was surrounded by tall chestnut trees and had a lovely gazebo in the centre when I was a child.

Our second home whose address was Stationsweg 24. My parents operated a profitable fruit and vegetable store there until we came to Canada. That house was situated outside De Wal and Ronald, Willy and I walked down the busy Steenstraat to go to school. Behind our home was a large garden where we had fruit trees, gorgeous flowers as well as a vegetable garden. There was also a lawn on which my mother would lay the white clothes after the wash was done, to have the sun bleach them. They had to be sparkling white! Our store faced the moat and I remember that after my Dad had a serious case of pneumonia, he went fishing there while recovering. Another vivid memory I have is that during the Tour de France a newsboy on his bicycle would careen around the corner at supper time screeching, "Tour de France! Tour de France!" with a newspaper giving that day's results of the etape. The men were anxiously awaiting him as they all had favourite competitors in that bicycle race. Much heated and excited discussion ensued from whatever the results were.

Our neighbours were a butcher named Kees Lust on one side and a small hotel owned by the Egermont Family on the other side. I vaguely remember being inside that hotel once but I don't remember much else about the people or the place. My mother told me that just after we moved there, Kees Lust ran over to get us to come and hide under his marble counter when there was some shelling going on just before the liberation.

It is incredible that whenever I am able to return to Hulst, the old buildings I recall from my childhood remain the same as they have been declared historic monuments. The façade cannot be altered but behind it some are quite different from its first incarnation. I feel immediately at home because of this. Preservation of old buildings is important to the Dutch people. The historical significance is honoured and appreciated. On the outskirts there are now many streets and structures which did not exist in my childhood. This is to be expected as the growth of the population necessitated new streets to accommodate the people.

Hulst will always have a most important place in my heart for as long as I live and I know I will return often. Arriving in Hulst from Schiphol Airport in Amsterdam is always very emotional for me.

hulst

map of inner city

Café in front, Basilica built between 1100 - 1200

Hulst Windmill built in 1792

BEHIND THE GREEN DOOR

OUR FIRST HOUSE had a very long address – Langebellingstraat 6, incongruous for such a humble abode. It was wedged between two grand houses, much larger and historically interesting.

The front door was a distinctive green colour with white trim and a transom window above. The little house had one double window in the living room overlooking the street. The stone (City Hall) Stadhuis, which sported a tall tower which is visible from great distances in this flat land, was located across the street from our home. The red tiled roof matched that of other houses in the walled city of Hulst in The Netherlands. There was a narrow hallway leading to a small kitchen at the back with a window looking out to a small grassy yard. Not many pictures were taken in those days, but there is one of me in the backyard.

My parent's bedroom had a dormer window on the second floor at the front of the house. This was the room in which I was born and 14 months later my brother Ronald as well. My parents turned the living room into a fruit and vegetable store since selling produce was something my mother had learned before she was married.

Our family moved to a larger place when I was 3, outside of the walled area of Hulst. The living areas were substantially more spacious and the added space meant that my parents could have a larger store as well.

When I was about 4 years old, somehow, I wandered away. I managed to find my way to the top of one of the massive cement gates which was an entrance to the inner city of our town. Someone spotted me sitting there. I was quite unconcerned – no fear in this little curious girl! This woman commented to my mother at the store that she had noticed a small child sitting on top of "De Bagijnepoort". My mother agreed with her customer that parents must take better care of their toddlers.

As the story was told, it was only when she came into the kitchen that she realised that I was missing. By this time my brother Willy had been born and with three little ones, the store, and the household to care for, it was no wonder that she had difficulty keeping track of her wandering small daughter. Frantically, she and a few neighbours, began to search. She finally remembered what her customer had said about a small girl sitting on top of one of Hulsts' massive concrete gates. Sure enough, it was me. My parents realised then that household help was needed and live-in Nanny Lona came into our lives to care for the young children and perform some housework.

When my Dad and I visited Hulst in September 1999, after Mom had died in March of 1997, to our surprise the little house with the green door was being torn down and it was totally demolished during our stay. The property had been purchased by a man named Tommy Stoorvogel an –acquaintance of my Uncle Guust. My uncle related to Mr. Stoorvogel my connection to that house. Subsequently, he came by my aunt and uncle's home bringing with him stones and bricks retrieved from the old place. He offered them to me but of course they were much too heavy to contemplate bringing them back to Canada. These stones told an interesting story. The large flat stones were several hundred years old and were from a convent that had been located there. That was startling information to us as even my father had never known that. Mr. Stoorvogel told us that the stones were quite valuable by this time. I took a photo of him with the retrieved stones and bricks. And so, we learned that our tiny house did have an interesting history after all. I have often wondered since then what other stories lay behind the little house with the green door where I was born.

My Father's Home, "de Langendam"

I HAVE SUCH fond memories of spending time at my father's home referred to as de Langendam in Hulst. My grandmother lived there, as did dad's sister Maria, her husband Remy and son Henny. The stone farmhouse was white–washed and could be seen as soon as we turned the corner of the road on our bicycles. We children always got excited as we really enjoyed going there!

My gentle, ailing grandmother's bedroom was on the main floor at the front of the house. She had a large window giving her a lovely view facing the road and the large lawn and flower gardens. The other bedrooms were upstairs. Before coming to Canada in 1951, we visited there every second Sunday. The other Sundays we visited my maternal grandparents, also on our bikes. What I remember most about sleeping in the farmhouse is the scent of the apples laid to dry on the attic floor just outside the room where I slept. Whenever I stayed there my Aunt Maria asked me to gather the warm eggs from under the hens. I loved doing that! She cooked me delicious eggs sunny-side up, always sunny- side—up every morning. The eggs always tasted appetizing, so flavourful.

In the yard there was the large pig pen. The pungent smell from the pigs was most unpleasant! I always hurried by as quickly as I could. The black and white cows were in the large brick barn and had to be milked morning and night but spent the rest of the time they grazing in the meadows. I could never get the hang of milking them but enjoyed watching the process and my Uncle Remy would squirt me with milk now and then to tease me. I think he did that because I was always talking—he was trying to get me to stop.

The filled milk buckets were taken to the summer -kitchen where the centerfuge sometimes called a separator, was located, to spin loudly to access the butter. The left - over milk was given to the pigs. The rest of the good milk was sold to customers who regularly came to de Langendam farm for milk and for fruit and vegetables, depending on the season. There was always something going on at the farm. There was another barn behind the brick one and this was where the hay was stored and where the farm horses were stabled.

Beside the house there was a big apple and pear orchard where it was fun for my brothers Ronald and Willy and I to play among the trees. Those apples were delectable! They were never sprayed so we could pull them right off the trees and eat them. Next, the enormous vegetable garden was located nearby. That was my Tante Maria's task and she enjoyed tending to the fruit and vegetables growing there. The garden was fertilized with manure. There was no shortage of that on the farm!

Everyone worked hard all week. On Sundays, however, they put on dress-clothes for church. In the afternoon the men played cards. The women enjoyed a peaceful cup of tea with cookies and chatted about family affairs. All enjoyed this day of rest. However, even on Sundays the cows had to be milked, pigs, hens and horses fed. There could never be a day off from those chores.

The fields had to be ploughed and seeded in the spring and there was hoe-ing going on regularly. In Autumn there was the harvesting of the hay and other crops. I remember a hand pump outside, close to the pig pen, where the men always washed their hands before going inside the house for meals. Their wooden shoes were lined up beside the door waiting for their owners' return. Wooden shoes are the best in the moist soil due to the high water table in Holland.

Their reputation as clean farmers had to be maintained as they never wanted to be called a vuilboer "dirty farmer." These farmers were considered lazy by the others. They did not pull the weeds growing between their plants and soon their plants were overgrown and became invisible. This inhibited their growth and produce.

Dad's brother, Bernard, had a farm across the large meadow from the family home. This gave my brothers and I the opportunity often to play with our cousins, Maurice, twins Mary and Marleen and their baby brother Freddy. Such fun!

My Dad, his three brothers, Charles, Frans, Bernard, and their sister Maria, were raised on this farm and loved it all their lives. Whenever my father travelled to Holland for a vacation, he needed to spend some time there and always did. There his Mother his sister and her family always welcomed him warmly.

I understood, from the time when I was quite young, what my father's life had been like before his marriage. He loved that farm, his home for many years, and referred to it often. Even though his life took other paths, he remained a farmer in his heart until the day he died.

The Langendam Farm

A Special Grandmother

SHE WAS THE kindest gentlest soul you could ever meet anywhere! Philomena Bruggeman de Burger was my Dad's stepmother but one would never know that she was not his biological mother. My father's biological mother, Julia Willaert de Burger died when he was just four years old, swept away in the Spanish Flu pandemic. Sadly, my father had no memory of her at all. When his father remarried several years later, Philomena took on the daunting job of raising four motherless little boys on a farm. She did this with love and encouragement and they all loved her equally in return. Some time later she gave birth to a baby girl named Maria and the boys were ecstatic to have a little sister! She treated all five of her children exactly the same way, with love and kindness.

When the grandchildren came along, she was our Mit, the same name we called my mother's mother. My memories of her as a child was of a tiny old lady invariably dressed in long dark dresses usually wearing a long, printed apron and always with a religious medal and/or a small brooch. Her dress style never varied. She always smiled her lovely smile as soon as she saw us and we felt her love palpably. She'd say, "Erna come and sit beside me and tell me about your friends". Those were such precious moments and still stand out clearly in my mind.

She became somewhat frail after the birth of her daughter Maria and my father often told of helping her by peeling potatoes even though he was no more than seven years old. The older boys had to help my grandfather with the farm chores. No one complained.

When we went to say goodbye to her before we immigrated to Canada, she had tears in her eyes and softly whispered, "I hope I will get to see you again some day." There were no recriminations to my parents for wanting to leave our country and go so far away.

The first time that I was able to return to Holland was in February of 1965, sadly for my maternal grandmother's funeral. I was an adult by this time, married with a baby daughter. After the funeral my mother and I went to De Langendam—the farm where my dad was raised and where my grandmother still lived now being cared for by her daughter Maria and her family. We were so very happy to see each other! Again, she asked in her soft voice, "Come and sit beside me, Erna, and tell me about your husband and baby girl Jacqueline." I was only too happy to oblige. I knew that her interest in me and my family was genuine. She really did want to know all about my life in far - away Canada.

My grandmother lived to the venerable age of 94. She died on December 8, 1973. She was in the nursing home in Hulst called "Blauwe Hoeve" at that time. Unfortunately, I was unable to attend her funeral as I was eight months pregnant with my youngest daughter, Allison. After her death when her will was probated, each of her five children received exactly the same inheritance. My Aunt Maria sent me her wedding ring which I will treasure all my life. Several years later when I went to Holland and had the opportunity to ask her why I had received this very special gift, her reply was simply, "You were the only one who asked for a souvenir of her. We had a family meeting and decided that you should have her wedding ring, also because you are the eldest de Burger granddaughter". I had the ring put on my charm bracelet as I did not want to take a chance on losing it. There it hangs along with other charms signifying events of my life which are important to me.

Generations

WHEN A PERIOD of time is referred to as a generation, it is generally accepted as being about 20 years. When we think of the next generation, we refer to those who come after us. So, that's my children Jacquie, Michelle, Allison. My nieces and nephews, David, Paul, Grace, Will, Kerry, Patrick, Joshua, Mallory, Kaleena. Next, it's our awesome grandchildren Emily, Rachel, Trent, Matthieu, Nicholas and if we're fortunate, we are given the gift of knowing our great grandchildren – in our case at present, Aayden.

When my mother was pregnant, my maternal great grandmother Camilla Thijs de Block, eagerly anticipated my birth hoping I would be a girl. This would make her the Matriarch of four generations of females. The fact that I was indeed a girl pleased her immensely. Her daughter, my grandmother, Emerentia de Block van den Branden, was also excited. They were so thrilled that when I was 16 months old, they took me to a professional photographer to record the event. This was in 1942 during the war! (In Dutch culture, to be considered a genuine four generations all must be of the same gender.) I have attempted to explain that even if the first child of any generation is a different sex, it is still 4 generations. I cannot convince my Dutch relatives that this is so.

As the years went on, I met and married Alex Fex and subsequently, my daughter Jacqueline was born making my grandmother, Emerentia van den Branden, the head of four generations. She was very pleased but sadly only lived three more months. I still have the letter she wrote me expressing her delight. As she lived in

Holland, she never got to see her first great grandchild, unfortunately, as she died soon thereafter.

In 1988, my daughter Michelle gave birth to Emily Susan McIntosh to our great elation. It was my mother, Alice van den Branden de Burger's turn to be a great-grandmother which made her very excited. Again, a new generation of our family had begun. Mom was enthusiastically interested in this new baby girl and couldn't wait to meet her. This happened when the baby was six weeks old. My parents lived in Wallaceburg which is an eight- hour drive from Sudbury. The happiness on her face told of her joy with this first great grandchild. When Emily was six years old, we had a professional photo taken which was very important to my mother, who was now the Matriarch of four generations of my maternal family.

My father became the head of four Generations of de Burgers in 1999 when Brennan was born. Brennan is the son of Will and Charlene de Burger and the grandson of my brother Frank de Burger. Dad didn't meet little Brennan until June of 2000 when he came to Sudbury for my graduation from Laurentian University (B.A.) and the wedding of his granddaughter, Grace de Burger and Mark Urbanski. Of course, pictures had to be taken to record this important event in the de Burger Family. No other de Burger Family in Holland was able to celebrate having four generations. Dad was the youngest son and the last of his family to pass away at the age of nearly 92.

The family circle continued as Emily McIntosh, our granddaughter, gave birth to Aayden Alexander Robidoux in 2009. The great euphoria and wonder I experienced completely infused me. My granddaughter had a baby! It was difficult to comprehend at first. As I held this little baby boy in my arms for the first time, it became a reality for me. Yes, he is male and is the beginning of the next generation in our family just the same. The proud matriarch of this new generation is me, Erna de Burger Fex! Just thrilling!

The thought that one day I would become a great grandmother never occurred to me when we began our family. Does Aayden make me feel old? Definitely not! I really enjoy our interactions. He knows and loves me as I love him and that makes me feel very happy. Spending time with him gives me (Oma) and his Opa so much joy!

1942 – Camilla Thijs de Block, Alice van den Branden de Burger,

Emerentia de Block van den Branden, Baby Erna de Burger (16 months old)

Four Generations of de Burgers

Frank, Florent, baby Brennan and Will de Burger 2000

Great grandmother – Alice de Burger, grandmother Erna de Burger Fex, Mother Michelle Fex, Emily McIntosh (6 years old)

Great grandmother Erna de Burger Fex, Grandmother Michelle Fex, Mother Emily McIntosh with Aayden

Robidoux (4 years old) 2013

Emily McIntosh with her son Aayden Robidoux

MY GREAT GRANDMOTHER
1878 — 1959

I AM A very fortunate woman. I had the opportunity to know and spend quality time with my Great grandmother Camilla Thijs de Block. We called her Opoe as was the custom in our part of The Netherlands. She evidenced her meaningful faith proudly. Camilla loved her family deeply and spent a great deal of time with my grandmother Emerentia van den Branden. Opoe wore her long hair in a bun on top of her head and was already gray when I was born when she was 63 years of age. Her clothes were long and always dark. My mother told me that her underpants were open in the centre as was common in those days in Holland. She loved her little brooches and always had one on her dress at the neck. Earrings in her pierced ears were the only other jewelry that she wore.

Opoe was born in 1878. Her husband Aloysius was born in 1874 and in 1939 was killed in a car accident having been hit by a doctor who was reputed to be drunk. Doctors were the only ones who owned cars then in our part of Holland. Camilla and Aloysius had 5 children namely: Emerentia (1896), Louis (1899), Irma (1904), Leonia (1906), Eugene (1908) and was grandmother to 15 grandchildren. Camilla was illiterate which was not uncommon for her generation.

Opoe loved going on pilgrimages to the Blessed Virgin Mary. There was a shrine in Northern Belgium in a small town called Boerijn where she attended regularly. Many rosaries were prayed there in honour of Mary. Since I was her first great - granddaughter she would take me with her at times. I loved being with her. But praying rosaries on my knees on those cobblestones hurt! Sometimes when we were at the shrine it might rain. She would deploy her large black umbrella for the two of us. Being so close to her under the umbrella was wonderful. My Opoe and I had a very special relationship. I loved her very much!

Attached to her small home, on the right was a little greenhouse where she grew green grapes. In the summer she pointed out the tiny grapes to me and we would check their progress whenever I came to stay at my Great Aunt Irma's home. Aunt Irma's home was attached to Opoe's home on the left of this tiny duplex. I loved her very much too, as well as her daughter, my second cousin Yvonne. When the green grapes were finally ripe, Opoe let me watch her pick some after lunch after which we enjoyed the sweet, tasty fruit.

Going to say goodbye to her in September of 1951, before our family's immigration to Canada, I don't know who cried more, she or me. Opoe died in 1959 at the age of 82 in the hospital in Hulst, so we never saw each other again. I was 18 years old at the time and living so far away in Canada made it impossible for me to attend her funeral in the Basilica in Hulst. She had been a widow for 20 years. I was very upset. I mourned her for a long time. She was such an important influence in my life. She was unforgettable! I was privileged to know her, love her, and be loved by her.

Great grandmother Opoe, with my grandparents Emerentia & Joseph van den Branden.

The Story of Alice — My Mother

MY MOTHER DID not have an easy life. Her love for her husband and children defined her. Her strong will, determination and her deep faith enabled her to survive challenges which would have overwhelmed most women.

Alice Camilla van den Branden was born in Hontenisse, Zeeland, The Netherlands on November 8, 1919. She was the second child, first daughter, of Joseph van den Branden and Emerentia de Block. Five more sisters, Louisa, Celina, Annie, Rachel and Corrie, and one brother followed her. The eldest of the family was her brother August (Gustaaf). Alice was named after her maternal grand-mother Camilla Thijs de Block. Alice attended school until she was 14 in Grade 8—and then even though she attained top marks, she had to leave school forever to help the family. This was common in the Depression Year of 1933.

Being the eldest daughter, meant that immediately many onerous responsibilities were thrust upon her slender shoulders. It never occurred to her to complain. Such was life at that time. Assisting with household chores such as laundry, cleaning, cooking was expected. The family also ran a small fruit and vegetable store so there was much to be done. Her father grew his own potatoes and other vegetables and it became Alice's job to accompany him to his rented field to harvest these before the store opened in the morning so that her mother could then sell the produce. Alice and her father left the house at four am to accomplish this. She often told me that she enjoyed this early morning work with her father and it drew them very close. She remained a morning person all of her life.

Alice met the love of her life, Florent de Burger, a young farmer, when she was 21, at a dance. They were married on February 14, 1941, in a civil ceremony at the town hall of St. Jansteen where her family was living at the time. The following day, February 15, they were married at the Catholic Church. This is the date they considered their anniversary. Alice wore a black dress as it was war and there was not much else to be found. She was 21 and Florent was 25. The young couple moved to Hulst and opened a small store in their living room. That store was very successful. Their first child, Erna, was born and 14 months later Ronald, arrived while they lived there. Alice now had two little children as well as the store to keep up with. Florent still worked part-time on his father's farm as well as in the store.

Feeling cramped, the time had come to search for a larger home for the family as well as bigger quarters for the store. Alice and Florent found just the right building close to the train station. The home section had 4 bedrooms, kitchen, living room and formal dining room, a spacious area for the store and a garage attached. It also had a large back yard for the children to play in and to grow fruit and vegetables. Alice was very happy here. Another son, Willy, was born on June 18, 1944. The war was nearly over in our part of Holland, and the whole family and the business flourished. Alice could afford a live-in housekeeper now to do the housework and look after her three small children. She loved working in the store six days a week, meeting people, and proved to have a real talent for business. When a salesman approached her about buying a large electric machine, which would peel and wash potatoes, carrots and other root vegetables she saw its merits immediately and she was right—her customers loved it and had their potatoes peeled and cleaned while they were chatting with her. The products for sale soon included staples such as sugar, salt, coffee, tea and many other things while still maintaining the designation of being a greengrocer. The law was strict about that in Holland. On February 15, 1948, a third son, Frank, named for Florent's deceased brother Frans, was born to Alice and Florent.

Florent had had the immigration "bug" since 1949 but Alice could not conceive of leaving her close-knit family and homeland to go somewhere where they did not know anyone nor the language or customs. His main concern was for the future of their three sons as he considered how devastated The Netherlands was after

WWII. His daughter (me) would just get married. Such was the thinking in the late 1940's. Eventually Florent's constant emphasis that where their future lay was in Canada, wore Alice down. Applications - reams of paper, were filled out for the family. Compulsory small pox vaccinations for the entire family were administered by the family doctor. Alice and Florent attended English classes in preparation for the major move. No one ever mentioned that Canadians also spoke French in some areas. Alice's father Joseph was very angry and upset and asked my mother to stay in Holland and let my father go alone to Canada if that is what he wanted. My grandfather said that he would help her look after her family. But as she explained later to me, "I had made my vows to your father and could not imagine being separated from him for an indefinite period of time. My place was with him and so was the children's." The building was sold, as was her lovely furniture. Our toys were given away to younger cousins and close friends. New warm clothes and thick blankets were purchased with the proceeds. Florent had applied to become a fruit farmer in Canada and was assured this would happen. My parents were given much misinformation that would directly impact their lives in Canada.

On October 2, 1951, after heart-wrenching goodbyes, Florent & Alice and their four children, boarded the ship "de Volendam" in the international port of Rotterdam. When we arrived in Warren, Ontario, on October 13, we were shocked to learn that we would be sharing a house with another Dutch family (Neeleman), who also had four children. My mother was very upset. We had not been told that this might happen. Tension was pervasive and Alice cried herself to sleep many nights feeling lonely for her parents, her homeland and so many other amenities that she had left behind. Then she discovered that she was pregnant when she began to hemorrhage. She could not speak English so it was difficult to explain her problems to the doctor who was summoned. He gave her to understand that she was to stay in bed for several weeks if she was to save this baby. To say that she was lonely was an understatement! In Holland her younger sisters would have come to her aid. Here there was no support except for my father. He had to work all day and the three older children went to school so she only had three year old Franky at home with her. Mrs. Neeleman and Alice did not get along as the other lady felt that her home had been invaded by this new family. This was not by our choice. The tension of living under the same roof with this woman and her family was unbearable to Alice.

An opportunity presented itself to my father to work on a farm in St. Charles where Florent would manage the farm while the owner Mr. Lafontaine would run the Red & White grocery store in the small town. After discussing this together Florent and Alice decided to make the move to the French-speaking town. The house that the farmer offered us was literally a shack. We could see out through the boards and rodents were everywhere. The only advantage was that we did not have to share this place with anyone. That was a relief to all of us but especially to Alice. However, within the first week of working there Florent sustained a serious accident. The bull charged him and gored him through the chest resulting in a badly broken elbow and arm, but miraculously missing all of Florent's major organs in his chest. He was hospitalized in Sturgeon Falls for about ten days. Alice was alone with her four children unable to visit him, as of course we had no car. Loneliness and isolation enveloped her also because she spoke neither English nor French. One of the neighbours took us to see my father on Easter Sunday at the hospital, a kindness much appreciated by the whole family.

When dad came home, he was unable to work due to his serious injuries. The money Alice and Florent had brought with them from Holland dwindled alarmingly quickly. One Sunday, Rev. Boyd from the Berean Baptist church in Sudbury arrived with his wife and a carload of clothes for all of us. We had no idea how he heard about us but for Alice it was humiliating to have to accept such charity. She told me later that if at that time they could have somehow scraped the money together to return to Holland they would have done so. She was much too proud, as was Florent, to even consider asking her father to send the fares for all of us, as he would have.

On June 6, Alice went into labour. Mr. Lemieux who lived on the next farm drove Alice and Florent to the hospital in Sturgeon Falls—the same hospital where my father had spent about ten days two months previously. The nun would not admit my mother, as dad's bill had not been paid. An unknown local gentleman generously paid dad's bill and so Alice was admitted. She gave birth to a daughter, Marianne, on my birthday June 7. I was ecstatic—finally a baby sister and on my birthday besides! As soon as Alice saw her new baby, her fifth, she realized that there would be problems with her. Marianne was a blue baby and had Down's Syndrome. However, mom came home with our precious Marianne. Florent was able to work on farms over the course of the summer after his huge cast was removed.

In August, a Dutch acquaintance who had a car told Florent that the mines in Sudbury were hiring and that the money was much better than working on the farm. The two men drove to Copper Cliff where Florent was weighed and hired immediately. He returned to St. Charles to tell Alice the good news. The one major drawback was that there were very few houses to rent in the Town of Creighton Mine where he was sent and he was expected to start work right away. And so, Alice was once again left alone this time with five children under 11, until her husband could find accommodation for the family. This took about six weeks. In the meantime, he lived in one of the Creighton boarding houses. The house he finally rented for us was two miles back of Creighton, an abandoned farm, literally in the bush. There were no neighbours, but the people of the Town of Creighton Mine welcomed us with open arms. Alice forever after referred to Creighton as our hometown in Canada. Father Regan, the parish priest, walked to visit Alice several times a week to have tea with her and to generally check to see how the family was faring. Miss Ursula Black, the school principal, as well as the other teachers, did everything they could to make us feel at home at Creighton Mine Public School. Parents of our schoolmates invited us to their homes for a hot lunch daily. Kindness and warmth were constantly in evidence. Carlo's Store as well as Fera & Celestini's store took turns bringing our groceries home for us—in the winter by horse and sleigh. Even though Alice was fearful living so far away from neighbours, especially with a sick baby, she did begin to feel at home in Canada somewhat. Sadly, Baby Marianne died just days before her first birthday, on June 4, 1952. Alice and Florent were devastated—to lose a child even though she had been ill, was an unimaginable pain. The birth of healthy baby Mary Alice (Liesje) on July 14, mitigated that pain a little but did not take it away. Nothing could do that. Creightonites Lando and Stella Vagnini graciously accepted when mom asked them to be godparents to our new baby Mary Alice. Father Regan baptized her at St. Michael's Catholic Church. He had also officiated at the funeral for Marianne and was most supportive of my parents.

In September, we moved into a house in Rockville (Dogpatch), near Creighton. Imagine - we had electricity, running water, only cold water, but what an improvement in our standard of living! We also had neighbours now, which made Alice very happy. Her "21 Club" of fellow women neighbours gave her a social life finally. She experienced sustained happiness for the first time in Canada. Florent built a small greenhouse and together they raised all kinds of plants which they later sold. The plants were of excellent quality and many Creighton residents drove out to purchase them. Alice absolutely enjoyed working in the greenhouse and selling the plants. Recently I met Helen Mynerich who reminded me that she used to come to purchase plants from my parents and how beautiful her flowers always were as a result. Catechism classes were held in our home for Catholic children from Rockville who attended public school. The teachers under the leadership of Miss Madelaine Rochon and Miss Blanche Gauthier prepared the children for First Holy Communion and Confession. For eight years life had normalcy for the whole family.

However, on Saturday March 12, 1960 the worst tragedy that could happen, did. Willy who was 15 at the time, received a phone call to set pins at the Mine-Mill Hall bowling lanes. Mom gave him permission to go, as this was one way that he and Ronald earned some spending money. Unbeknownst to us he decided to take his bike ......and almost directly in front of our house was hit by a drunk driver at 8:15 pm. He died at 10:15 pm of his severe injuries. A healthy son, his life snuffed out so quickly! Alice and Florent were speechless in their grief! Now they had lost two children. Again, Creightonites showed their love and many kindnesses by attending the funeral Mass, bringing food and making many visits to our home. Father Regan, Miss Black, Stella Vagnini, Maria Bruyns and many others were frequent visitors in the difficult days and weeks afterwards giving my mother the support she needed while Dad was at work and we were at school.

After this Alice could no longer remain in this home where she had been so happy. The kitchen window above the sink, where she stood to prepare her meals and wash her dishes, looked out at the spot where this horrendous accident had occurred. Baby Lillian was born on April 24, 1960, after a most difficult labour for Alice. Due to the horrific emotional upheavals that Alice had experienced, she developed a very serious fever and was extremely ill and bed-ridden. She was hospitalized a full month before she was well enough to return home to her family. Alice was 41. My parents decided that they must sell this house. It was filled with too many heartbreaking memories. Their next-door neighbours Allan and Patsy Green purchased it. In January of 1961, Alice and Florent moved to Whitefish where they opened and operated a convenience store for 11 years. For the first two years Florent continued to work at Creighton Mine. On Boxing Day of 1962, he sustained a massive heart attack while working underground. Alice was shocked, fearing whether he could survive this. Dr. McGruther told her that we would have to wait a week before he could tell us for sure. What next, was Alice's thought? Florent was hospitalized at Copper Cliff Hospital for five weeks where he received excellent care. He was unable to return to work at the mine for seven months. Another setback! In 1966 he received a disability pension from INCO after having suffered another heart attack. Alice and Florent were grandparents by this time to my daughter Jacquie which was a role they absolutely loved. They were called Mit & Pit, a common custom in Holland.

Alice lost her mother in February of 1965 and with Erna, went to Holland for the funeral—a most difficult trip. Both Florent and Alice operated the Whitefish store until 1969 when they decided that they wanted to move to Southern Ontario. They had visited a lovely town named Wallaceburg where they discovered that many people from their hometown of Hulst in The Netherlands were living.

And so, in June of 1969 they moved there with 16 -year - old Liesje and 9- year-old Lillian. They again operated a convenience store which was open seven days a week until their retirement in 1979 when Alice was 60 years old. She had been working since she was 14. A different opportunity presented itself then. This one she took on with pleasure. The Welcome Wagon in Wallaceburg needed a representative—would she be interested? With her excellent people skills, she excelled and won an award of recognition in the form of a lovely plate. She was so very proud of that! She did this job for seven years joyfully and loved every day.

In December of 1991, Alice became very ill. She was hospitalized first in Wallaceburg, then in London where she underwent many tests over a period of nearly a month. Dad and I drove to see her daily. The diagnosis was not good. She had cirrhosis of the liver and the specialist estimated that she had possibly five years to live. It was genetic with four of her sisters also having suffered liver problems. Alice grew progressively weaker with time, and was hospitalized several more times. She became so weak eventually that she had to go to a nursing home called Lapointe—Fisher which was right on Nelson Street where her home was. Florent and Alice's 56th Wedding Anniversary was on February 15, 1997, but she was barely aware of it. The entire family had been summoned at this time and we prayed around her bed and expressed our love and appreciation to her. I'll never forget her grasping my dad's arm, looking him right in the eye and asking, "Is it really so far?" "Ja, mens," he said with tears in his eyes. She slipped into a coma shortly after that and passed away on March 3 at the age of 76. Her five children survived Alice, also her twelve adored grandchildren, Jacquie, Michelle, Allison, David, Paul, Will, Grace, Kerry, Patrick, Joshua, Mallory and Kaleena and two much-loved great—granddaughters, Emily and Rachel, as well as her beloved husband. She left us a legacy of unconditional love of family, an example of the importance of hard work, and a clear sense of priorities in life.

At her funeral, family friend Father Dikran Islemeci, told us the strength of her faith had been an inspiration to him on the many occasions that he visited Alice. Her grandchildren honoured her by being pall—bearers, doing the readings and being flower—bearers. She would have been proud to see her family all together being supportive of dad and of each other.

Wedding picture Florent & Alice de Burger

February 15, 1941

Alice—her favourite photo – smiling

Her children 1949 – Ronald, Willy, Franky and Erna

SINT NICHOLAAS

GROWING UP AS a small child in Holland I anxiously waited for the first week in December as mysterious things began to happen at our house in Hulst. We heard a sharp knock at the door, then a white gloved hand appeared around the door magically, throwing spicy round cookies into the room. All of us would scramble to see who could get the most. Mom always made us give some to our little brother Franky because he couldn't get as many as Ronald, Willy and I. We didn't really mind as he couldn't eat very many anyway. My brothers and I were very excited! Sinterklaas was coming!!

Our parents informed us that Sint Nicholaas, or Sinterklaas as we called him, had arrived in the international port of Rotterdam by steamship from Spain with his two black helpers called Zwarte Piet. It was true—he was really in our country! We sang many songs about him of which I only remember one, namely, " Zie gindst komt de stoomboat uit Spanje weer aan; Het brengt ons Sint Nicholaas, ik zie hem al staan, Hoe huppelt het paardje (horse) het dek op en neer, Hoe waaien (by the wind) de wimpels (streamers) heen en al weer..." Every Dutch child knows that one! That Sunday, we actually saw him riding on his white horse through our town. He was a very imposing figure dressed in his red robe with a tall mitre on his head and staff in his hand, like a bishop. He had a long white beard and long white hair too. White gloves covered both hands. All the children and their parents were lined up along his route frantically waving and yelling our welcome to him. The two Zwarte Piets walked along both sides of the street handing out the spicy cookies to all. This happened in all towns and cities on the same day but we were too young to understand how he could be all over the country on the same day.

Several days before December 6, we would begin to receive small gifts from Sinterklaas, sometimes with little notes attached telling us to be sure to behave before the big night. We would leave our shoes by the fireplace with hay or carrots for his horse. In the morning, the shoes were empty so we knew that Sinterklaas was happy with us. The evening of December 5 we put our Dad's wooden shoes (they were the biggest) by the fireplace along with a note asking for our most desired gifts. We went to bed early because that way morning would come faster (we thought). Of course, it was difficult to fall asleep. For the adults it was the enjoyable pakjes avond. They had wrapped up little parcels (pakjes) to which funny rhymes were attached directed at the receiver of the little gifts. Naturally glasses of wine and other beverages were consumed causing the evening (avond) to result in great hilarity for all of them.

On the morning of December 6, we rushed downstairs to discover what Sinterklaas had brought us. When I was 8 years old, I received a small blackboard on an easel with chalk and a brush—exactly what I had hoped for! He always brought me a book as well because somehow, he knew that I liked to read. We each received our initial in chocolate too, as our parents did. That was traditional. I was very happy and excited. There was a message from Sint Nicholaas on that blackboard telling me that since I was the eldest, I must try to be a little better behaved with my younger brothers next year. I have to admit to running out of patience with the three of them at times. How did he know? I was the only girl and so was expected to take care of them for short periods of time once in a while. My dolls never complained and always listened to me. It was much more fun to play with them. My parents always put up a Christmas tree close to December 25th. It was a real tree decorated with little candles which my father lit carefully, warning us not to come too close. One year that tree caught fire and Dad threw it outside into our little courtyard and doused it with a pail of water. I was really frightened! Every Christmas Mom put out the stable with the little Nativity statues, celebrating the Birth of the Baby Jesus. The familiar Christmas hymns in the Basilica rang out as the acoustics in that ancient church are excellent. Such precious memories!

In 1951, after we came to Canada, all of our Sint Nicholaas customs changed completely, in fact, disappeared. My parents had no siblings with whom to enjoy pakjes avond. Apparently Sinterklaas had not heard of our leaving our homeland as there were no presents on the morning of December 6, St Nicholaas Day. We learned from our school mates that the children received presents in Canada on Christmas Day, December 25th! How strange that seemed to us that first year. Due to our family having very little money, we received one present for all four of us, a sleigh. We had never experienced snow in Holland. After attending Christmas Mass in Warren at St. Thomas Catholic Church, Mom cooked a delicious dinner for all of us. Although it was a very cold day, we played outside with our sleigh all day. That was fun for us but I know it was a sad, lonely day for my parents so far way from their families.

I have continued the tradition of buying chocolate letters for our family including my nieces and nephews. Sometimes an initial may be sold out so I have had to be creative but everyone enjoys the tradition of receiving them (and eating them). The last several years, I have hosted the family to a day of making & partaking of oliebollen. Oliebollen are like deep fried donuts which the family dips into icing sugar and LOVES to eat!!

In 2020, a year of so many challenges, my grandson Trent called to let me know he was going to buy the chocolate letters for the entire family. It was such a generous offer and I was deeply touched by this kindness.

Sinterklaas

IMMIGRATION JOURNEY

ONCE AGAIN, I could hear my mother crying in the night. I jammed the pillow over my head to drown out that awful sound. My own tears kept falling as well. Loneliness, isolation, fears—are common feelings of an immigrant on a ship taking us to an unknown land. I was only 10 years old, but I remember it vividly. We had boarded the huge ship "De Volendam" in Rotterdam on October 2, 1951. The heartbreaking goodbyes to grandparents, aunts, uncles, cousins and friends, our home, culture and language, were painful. However, my three brothers and I were very excited walking up the gangplank amid fifteen hundred other immigrants all leaving Holland for Canada.

One morning a voice on the public address system advised us to look to the right of the ship and our gazes were met by the breath-taking panorama of enormous icebergs rising from the sea. We shivered in the cold and the bright sun made them sparkle as though encrusted with crystals. On another day, incredibly, we observed whales seemingly dancing in the waves.

Unfortunately, sea sickness for Dad and one of my brothers, made the journey more difficult. This, coupled with the fact that our family had been separated upon boarding, made us feel uneasy. Dad and two of my brothers, Ronald and Willy, were sleeping in the large, dark hold, and mom and I and my three-year-old brother Franky, shared a tiny, stuffy cabin. Bunk beds and a small toilet and sink were all the furnishings it contained. One day I left the cabin to get some fresh air and to play with my brothers on deck. Upon my return, I discovered that my new book with a white kitten on the cover, had been stolen! It was the only book I had been allowed to bring in my little red suitcase. I had placed it under my pillow before leaving the cabin and couldn't believe that anyone could be so mean! I was devastated! Mom promised to buy me a new one as soon as we were settled in our new home not realizing that the books in Canada would be in English, a language I could not read.

We arrived in Quebec City on a glorious, fall day, October 11. We had been sailing for nine days. After going through innumerable immigration and vaccination checks we were taken to a train going to Montreal. With great difficulty, we had to change trains there to get to Warren in Ontario. On the train, we tasted Pepsi Cola for the first time. I didn't like it. We arrived in Warren two days later, tired but happy that our trip was over and anxious to see our new home. Dad's employer, a dairy farmer named Mr. Spaull, was to meet us but he was not at the station. Each time a man entered the station Dad would show him our papers to ask if he was Mr. Spaull. Finally, a tall man entered and conveyed to us that he had been sent to pick us up and that he was Mr. Spaull's brother-in-law. Unbelievably, we children had to ride in the back of his pick-up truck to our new home. That new home was a major disappointment! We were dismayed to realize that we would be sharing this two-storey house with an unknown Dutch family, also with four children—the Neelemans. Just imagine- four adults and eight children under ten, sharing one three-bedroom house. Extreme loneliness and feeling disconnected were constants.

Another Dutch family, the Terpstra's, had already been in Canada for 2 years and so were fairly fluent in the English language. We learned a lot from them. Our first teacher, Miss Seguin, found us to be ahead of her students in mechanical math. It was imperative that we focus on learning the English language before we could advance in our other studies. Whenever she had any free time, Miss Seguin would teach us words by having us do the actions. "Turn, Erna", she would say. We also learned on the playground from the other pupils. We children learned the language quickly and this was helpful for our parents. Dad was learning rudimentary English at the farm where he was working. However, since most of the other men were immigrants from several different countries, actions often spoke louder than words which led to hilarious misunderstandings. Children often learn a new language easier than their parents and become the translators for their parents. This is not uncommon for many immigrant families.

It was most difficult for Mom at home with three—year—old Franky. She had little contact with the outside world and thus she was extremely lonely. One day she needed bleach for our clothes and sent me to the store in town. I walked the half hour to Warren worrying how I was going to find what she needed. I searched all around the store and finally a kind saleslady approached me and asked me what I needed. With words and actions, I managed to convey mom's request. As soon as she understood, she found it for me. I was so happy that I rushed and sang all the way home with the bleach. My parents were very proud of me.

de Burger Family before boarding in Rotterdam
In front – Erna, Franky, Willy-at the back Dad (Florent) Mom (Alice) and Ronald.

Ship, de Volendam

Immigrant Challenges

HAVE YOU EVER stopped to consider the numerous problems facing immigrants arriving in Canada? It is indubitably a wonderful country with so many opportunities. That is the reason that people from so many other lands have chosen to leave their homeland to make a new life here. Most immigrants feel apart as they have left family and a strong support network behind. For our family it was indeed a life-changing event!

Destitution was very familiar to immigrants. The small amount of money Dad had been allowed to bring to Canada soon disappeared in taking care of necessities. The lack of extended family, language problems, loneliness, not understanding the culture and customs, isolation, made the first two years very difficult for the de Burger family and many others.

There was a very steep learning curve for new immigrants. Our Dutch meals consisted of soup, meat, potatoes, vegetables and fruit for dessert, never bread with the hot meal. We missed having fish several times a week. We were very surprised to learn that Canadians exchanged gifts at Christmas and not on December 6 as in Holland.

We didn't have the proper clothing for frigid Canadian winters. I well remember wearing two coats to school, two pairs of mittens, and tall felt boots purchased in Warren. These boots were not pretty but they were warm and we were glad to have them! We were totally unprepared for the mountains of snow that fell that winter too. We had seldom seen snow in Holland but here it we were surrounded by it and we children loved playing in it. Those tall felt boots kept our feet dry. The boots had a rubber shoe over them which we removed.

Another problem was that we had been able to bring very little furniture to Canada in the *kist*. This was a huge wooden box which was filled with miscellaneous items that our parents had chosen carefully to bring. Only many blankets, kitchen tools, a kitchen table, some pictures, and new clothes for all. There were a few sentimental items such as the crucifix that hung above my parents' bed and remained there until the death of my father in 2007. No toys were brought to Canada and I really missed my wicker doll carriage!

My parents were strict and that was all we knew. However, as we began to make friends with kids our own age, we became aware of the different lifestyle of Canadian families. I wanted us to be just like my Canadian friends. This caused some conflict in our home. Many times, I felt that I did not fit in. For me that feeling recurred for many years. We were living between two worlds. "Uprooted" explains exactly how I felt.

St. Charles Days (1952)

OUR PARENTS HAD high hopes when we moved to St. Charles from Warren. Through Dr. Seguin, the Warren veterinarian, Dad had met with Mr. Jean Lafontaine of St. Charles. Mr. Lafontaine owned a farm but was planning to operate the Red & White grocery store in the village. He needed someone to work his farm and all that this entailed. The arrangement was that the person would work into a partnership of the farm. Therefore, if a cow had two calves for instance, one belonged to my father and the other to the owner. Dad had been born and raised on a farm in The Netherlands and our parents saw the opportunity to build up a farm themselves with this arrangement.

Consequently, the family moved to St. Charles into a "house" provided by the farmer. What a disappointment that dwelling was! We could literally see outside through the cracks in the walls. It really was not much more than a shack. The only redeeming feature was that we were living by ourselves instead of with another family. However, within the first week of Dad's employment, a bull charged at him and gored him through the chest as the animal rolled my father on the ground with its horns. Miraculously all his major organs were missed, however he did sustain a badly broken arm and elbow. My father was taken to the hospital in Sturgeon Falls and was admitted for about 10 days. When he came home, he was sporting a large and heavy cast. The worst result of the accident meant that he could not work. My brothers Ronald (9) and Willy (7) did some of the chores that Dad was unable to accomplish.

With Dad being not being able to work, the little money they had been allowed to bring with them from Holland, was soon depleted. Since our Dad was not able to perform his duties, someone else had to be hired. These were difficult days for our family especially for our parents. My mother cried often at night.

Another Dutch family worked on a different farm in St. Charles. The man spoke to his employer and since Dad's cast was gone, he was able to work there. We moved again. The house provided there was a little better than the previous one. St. Charles days were most unhappy for our family. We had not yet been in Canada a full year and had had to relocate three times.

Marianne

Mom couldn't understand why she was constantly feeling unwell in November 1951. However, with the sea voyage to Canada, and the painful farewells to her family, she felt it was due to all these difficult events. Spontaneously, in November she started to bleed. Here they were in a strange land where neither of my parents spoke the language, had no family support nor did they know any doctors. My Dad explained to his employer that a doctor was needed as quickly as possible for his wife. When the doctor arrived, we were scared. We did not understand what was wrong with our Mom. The doctor gave my parents to understand that Mom was pregnant and if the baby was to be saved, she must stay in bed for the next several weeks. My parents had to pay him in cash. So, as the eldest, I needed to learn to do many household tasks.

After moving to St. Charles, in early June 1952, Mom went into labour. The nearest hospital was in Sturgeon Falls 20 miles away. A neighbour, Mr. Lemieux, drove mom and dad to the hospital. As the back roads were not paved, it was a terribly difficult ride for my mother. When they arrived at their destination Mom was in hard labour. Dad approached the nun at the registration desk to ask that mom be admitted. She refused, telling Mr. Lemieux that Dad's hospital bill must be paid first. A man happened to walk into the hospital lobby, took in the situation at a glance and asked the Sister what the problem was. After it was explained to him, he took out some money, paid dad's hospital bill and finally Mom was admitted. This man refused to give Dad his name and we never did find out who this "angel" was.

After a very difficult labour, my Mom gave birth to Baby Marianne. This was Mom's fifth child and as soon as she saw her, knew that there was something very wrong with this baby. The most obvious was her colour. She was a "blue" baby, not the natural pink of other babies. Also, Mom noticed that her eyes were somewhat slanted and realized right away that Marianne was mongoloid—later known as a Down Syndrome child.

Marianne was born on June 7, my 11th birthday! When Dad arrived home to tell us that we had a baby sister, I was elated! Finally, after three brothers I had a baby sister, and on my birthday! Dad apologized to me as he had only a small birthday gift for me, a red, white and blue sponge ball. Joyfully I replied that I had received the best present possible for my birthday, a baby sister.

That evening Mrs. Lafontaine invited us for supper. Her sister was there as well. I had excitedly told this other lady about our new baby and how anxious I was for my mother to bring Marianne home. The two women were speaking to each other in French with concerned looks on their faces. By this time, I understood enough French to realize they were discussing the fact that, "le bebe est tout bleu". The expressions on their faces told me that the baby might not be coming home with my mother. Fear lodged in my heart. However, it dissipated when a week or so later mom did indeed bring our new baby girl home.

Marianne had red curly hair and big blue eyes. She was beautiful!

She was baptized when she was about 3 weeks old. The priest spoke only French and my parents only a little English. My brother Ronald and I had learned enough French to communicate with the priest and so the baby was christened. The priest made no effort to speak with my parents. This ceremony was necessary but not joyful as previous family baptisms had been. My parents felt hurt and insulted.

When Marianne was three months old, we moved to Creighton Mine where my father was working in the mine. The baby was often ill. The doctor explained to my parents that the baby was multiply- handicapped physically and mentally. Creighton residents drove Mom and Dad to hospital each time it was needed. One day while working underground, one of Dad's colleagues asked,"Dutchie, I heard that you have a sick baby". He told him about a hospital in Toronto that was just for sick children. That day on the way home from work, Dad stopped in to ask Dr. McGruther, the Creighton doctor, whether Marianne could be helped there. Dr. McGruther replied that she was not strong enough to survive the train trip and advised my parents to keep her at home and care for her the best way they could.

In May of 1953, Father Moore came to Creighton with the statue of Our Lady of Fatima with which he travelled the world. After hymns and prayers around the statue near the church, Father Regan told Father Moore about our family. The two priests walked to our home, bringing with them the rosary from the statue. After we prayed the rosary around Marianne's bassinette, Father Moore gave my mother a small blue medal he took off his watch and asked to Mom pin it to the baby's nightie. He also said that we should pray and promised we would see a change in her condition within ten days. On the tenth day Marianne died. What a shock! I will never forget watching my Mom putting a mirror in front of the baby's mouth to see if she was still breathing. She was not. Dad had sent my brother Ron on his bike for the doctor. Dr. Thibodeau pronounced the baby dead. Mom washed her, then wrapped her in a blanket and Dad carried her in his arms out of the bush. When he got to Wavell St., Mr. Douglas Brown was in his front yard and asked if he could help. Dad explained that his baby was dead. Mr. Brown drove Dad to Lougheed's Funeral Home, on Eyre St. in Sudbury. The next day, June 5, we had a small funeral service for her conducted by our parish priest, Father Regan. I will never forget that small white casket. I will never forget her. Marianne was 3 days shy of her first birthday. In her short life she had drawn our family closer together.

Erna 11, Marianne 2 weeks, Mom Alice

CREIGHTON, MY HOMETOWN

PEOPLE OFTEN ASK me why I am so attached to the Town of Creighton when I was not born there. It's true. I was not even born in Canada. But when our family arrived in Creighton in 1952, living on an abandoned farm two miles behind the town in fact, Creightonites received us with open arms and hearts.

It began with Miss Ursula Black, principal of Creighton Mine Public School. When Dad took us to register at the school, she could not have been kinder to my father, me, Ron and Willy. She placed me in Grade 5 with Mr. Keith MacNaughton, Ron in Grade 4 with Mrs. Rita Craigen and Willy with Miss Ann McClelland in Grade 3. All of the teachers assisted us in every way possible. This was appreciated because we spoke only rudimentary English as we had been in Canada less than a year. We really appreciated that the children on the playground included us in their games from the first day.

Father Emmett Regan made us most welcome at St. Michael's Catholic Church. Accompanied by his dog, he often walked to visit my mother during the week for tea. She was at home alone with my little brother Franky and our baby sister Marianne who had Down Syndrome. Mom loved his visits. His big Irish smile always perked up her day. Sometimes parishioners invited us for breakfast after Sunday Mass, all six of us! I remember Mrs. Eileen Massey hosted us several times. Often Mrs. Reid invited my two brothers and me for a hot lunch usually tomato soup and delicious grilled cheese sandwiches. The first time I tasted pumpkin pie was at the home of our choir director, Mrs. Della Drennan. It was so good and I've loved it ever since.

In August 1953, Stella and Lando Vagnini invited all of us to their grand wedding at the Caruso Club in Sudbury. There were six bridesmaids each wearing long gowns in rainbow colours. My parents had never experienced an Italian—Ukrainian marriage celebration and found it breathtaking especially when the guests lined up to kiss the bride and then put money into a container after doing so. My parents were accustomed to the much smaller Dutch weddings where the guests were all family members.

In 1960, when my brother Willy, 15 years old, he was killed in a car accident, and the support of Creightonites was overwhelming. So much food was brought to our home that it was impossible for our family to consume it all. Stella Vagnini cooked a delicious chicken dinner at our home while we were gone to the funeral. Miss Black came to visit us on several occasions as did Father Regan, numerous times. St. Michael's was packed for the funeral Mass. Many Creightonites had come to the funeral home as well even though we didn't know them.

The Ladies' Auxiliary of the church organised a huge baby shower for Mom and our new baby Lillian who was born just 6 weeks after my brother's accident. My mother was invited to become a member of the Ladies' Auxiliary which she did happily and enjoyed the association with the ladies of the parish. Creightonites included us in every aspect of the life of the town.

My teaching career began at Creighton Mine Public School in 1962, the school I had attended as a child. That was a special thrill for me. I was living at the Teachers' Residence on Snider St. with most of the staff which facilitated us becoming well acquainted and indeed becoming friends, friendships which have lasted until today.

When Alex and I got married on December 28, 1963, it was the Ladies Auxiliary of St. Michael's church who catered our wedding dinner in Cabrini Hall located beside the church, even though it was during the busy season between Christmas and New Year's. Creighton well-wishers gave us many lovely gifts. We moved into an apartment at 27 George St. across the street from the school, most convenient for me. Our eldest daughter, Jacqueline Marianne, was born while we resided there.

We then moved to Wavell St. where the neighbours were like family. Everyone looked out for all the children. Our second daughter, Michelle Joanna, was born during the years we lived there. Bringing two babies into our homes in Creighton Mine definitely made the town feel like our home town.

Dad worked underground at the mine in Creighton which is why our family had moved to the little town. Colleagues explained safety factors to him as working deep underground was a totally new experience for this man who had been born and raised on a farm in The Netherlands. He had never envisioned working in a mine but he needed money to support his family in this new country.

Unfortunately, the Town of Creighton no longer exists due to the mining company's plans to divest itself of residential real estate but in 1989 the first exhilarating Creighton Reunion, called "Creighton Shines in '89" was held. The excitement was palpable everywhere on the town site. Creightonites came literally in the thousands from many places in Canada and the United States. Huge tents were erected to accommodate the people. Since then, Creighton Reunions have been held every year on the 3rd Sunday of September with 2019 being the 30th Annual Creighton Reunion. I have received phone calls and email messages from Alberta, Saskatchewan, Manitoba, New Jersey and many places in Ontario asking about the upcoming reunion. I advertise the annual reunions every year with posters, flyers and on social media inviting anyone who ever lived in Creighton to come once again to reconnect with former neighbours and friends. Due to the world-wide pandemic a physical 31st reunion was impossible in 2020. But, talented Creightonite Audrie Jamieson Brooks organized a successful virtual reunion.

The physical Town of Creighton has been gone since 1986 but the Spirit of Creighton lives on and flourishes in our memories. My home town in Canada will always be Creighton Mine because of the warm welcoming people of that small town.

Creighton Mine - Old picture—log cabin and houses

Creighton Mine Train Station (school in the background.)

Picking Blueberries

WHILE OUR FAMILY was living in the bush in 1952-3, Mom noticed many people approaching our house early in the morning, then go into the bush and climb up on the hills surrounding the area. Several hours later they would re-emerge carrying full baskets of blueberries. We knew nothing about this activity at the time as it was only our second summer in Canada. Dad asked one of his colleagues at the mine about this. He learned that these Creightonites were picking blueberries which grew wild on the hillsides, to send away to Toronto which assisted them to earn some extra money. He and Mom decided that we would do this too. My parents had been searching for some way of earning some extra funds in order that they could save enough money to enable them to purchase a house. The family needed to move out of the bush into an actual neighbourhood where we would not be so lonely and isolated in this new land.

Creighton Mine was a multi-ethnic town which we did not realize when we moved here. Blueberry season brought that home to us as we witnessed ladies emerging from the forest carrying full baskets on their heads. We children were amazed and could not help staring as we had never before witnessed such an unusual sight. Often these ladies would ask mom for a drink of water before going home as it was extremely hot on the hillsides. They would put their 11- quart baskets down and rest for a few minutes while consuming the water. As we watched in fascination this one particular lady who picked daily, would place a round wooden disk on the scarf on her head, adjust it, then carefully put her 11- quart basket on top of that disk. After that she would bend her knees carefully and pick up her two other baskets of blueberries to carry them to her home in Creighton. We never saw her spill any berries as she went on her way! Her accent was difficult to understand but we eventually discovered that she had immigrated from Croatia. We never did learn her name—but she was a welcome daily visitor throughout blueberry season.

Dad took my two brothers, Ronald and Willy and myself up into the hills early one July morning to see if we could find the berries we had heard so much about from others. Since it was our first foray into the woods, we carried all manner of containers with us. It did not take us very long to locate a wonderful spot absolutely filled with the low bushes bearing copious amounts of berries! Quickly we sat down and began to pick but many little branches and leaves fell into our pails as well. My brother Willy, who was only 8 years old, decided that he would sooner eat blueberries than put them into his container. They were undeniably delicious but his pail was not filling. Our Dad noticed that Willy's mouth, tongue and hands were stained a give-away blue revealing what had been happening. Dad soon put a stop to that and insisted we must fill our various containers before we could return home. From then on, picking blueberries became our daily routine. When Dad was working afternoon shift, we left the house early in the morning returning home in time for him to wash, eat and walk to work at the mine. The following week he worked day shift and we climbed the hills in search of blueberries after an early supper. Mom stayed home with 4- year- old Franky and our baby sister Mary Alice. Occasionally she would go with Dad and my brothers in the evening while I babysat the little ones. By questioning his colleagues at work, Dad soon learned about the proper baskets, covers and how to ship our berries to Toronto by train as many other Creightonites were doing. From then on, he carried our baskets with him to work and dropped them off at the Creighton train station.

Our father grasped blueberry picking skills very quickly and was soon able to pick an 11-quart of the small blue wonders in good time. He even figured out how to find a hilly spot on a windy day to clean the berries by letting the breeze blow out the detritus. This was essential as more money was paid by Stronach in Toronto for blueberries in excellent condition. Picking these little blue beauties was, and is, hot difficult work. It takes many berries to fill an 11 quart or even a 6 - quart basket which is what we were expected to pick. However, our efforts were poorly rewarded during the height of the season when the cheques would arrive paying a meager $4.00 for an 11quart basket of blueberries.

However, by the end of that first season we had accomplished our goal and my parents had saved enough money for a down payment on a house in Rockville aka Dogpatch. All of our efforts towards this end were rewarded by being able to move into a house in a built-up area with the luxury of electricity(!). The lesson we children learned was a valuable lifelong one! Hard work brings results! And wild blueberries are delicious!

Blueberries

GRATITUDE

ON A DARK December night in 1952, there was a knock on our door. Since we lived literally 2 miles from our nearest neighbour, we were all somewhat apprehensive. My father answered the door and there stood Father Regan, our parish priest and two other men. These "angels" had a sleigh full of toys and food for our family. We could not comprehend why this was happening as our English was still very poor. We had been in Canada for 14 months. Father Regan helped us to understand that these were gifts for our family with no expectations (no strings attached).

I remember very well that they gave me a doll whom I immediately recognised as Snow White. She was beautiful! She had black hair, a lovely face and was wearing a long blue skirt, a yellow top with an orange velvet cape over the dress. I know that my three brothers also received presents but I don't remember what they were. For my parents, the best gifts of all were all the ingredients for a festive Christmas Dinner. There was a large ham, oranges, grapes, apples and other food stuff—but I don't remember if there was a turkey. We sincerely thanked the two men and Father Regan. It must have been he who told these people about our family.

The following year we were living in our own house in Dogpatch—a small settlement between Creighton Mine and Lively. As time went on my Dad purchased a black and white television set. Dad and the boys loved watching sports on TV. One Saturday, a program came on and I figured out that people were promising to send money to help those in need. After several years of watching this annual broadcast well into the night, I realised that our family had been a beneficiary in 1952. I learned that an organisation called the "Lions Club" fulfilled all those Christmas wishes and delivered the gifts to the families whose names had been submitted to them. It was an ambitious task that they handled with handshakes, smiles and good will.

As long as I have been working and earning money, I always donated to their annual Telethon, understanding how they help families as we had experienced. I will never forget that knock on the door so long ago which made our Christmas so wonderful! I will feel immense gratitude to the Lions Club as long as I live. Thank you to the Lions Club for this wonderful work.

LIFE IN DOGPATCH

DOGPATCH (AKA ROCKVILLE) is a small community located between the towns of Creighton Mine and Lively. In September 1953, when we moved into our own house, we were so excited! To be moving into a community was a goal accomplished! My mother especially had been extremely lonely living in the bush. She soon had friends and the ladies formed a club called "The Twenty—One Club" as there were 21 original members. They met in each other's homes once a month for fellowship and fun and Alice looked forward to those meetings with pleasure. She now had a social life.

We settled in quickly. Our new home had two-storeys with three bedrooms upstairs. Since I was the only girl, I got a bedroom of my own. My three brothers, Ronald, Willy and Franky shared the largest bedroom and our parents and Baby Mary Alice (Liesje) had the other one. Later, when Liesje was older, she slept with me in my double bed. I loved having my little sister sleeping with me! We had an outhouse, which we had experienced at the house in the bush so that was no big deal. I was the oldest of seven children and female so many chores were assigned to me. (I hated darning socks and ironing!) Ronald and Willy had to help our Dad with various duties. None of us ever thought about complaining. There was also a garage where our bicycles and other superfluous things were stored

Our Dad built a greenhouse in which he planted seeds to grow into plants which he sold. Many Creightonites came to buy those plants and raved about the beauty of their flowers and healthy vegetables.

It didn't take us long to make friends. My closest friends were; Verna Spencer, Barbara Green, Lorraine Mead and Betty Makela. We were all about the same age, so it was easy to find activities we all enjoyed.

There was a one-room schoolhouse which we all attended. Mrs. Agnes O'Brien taught all the grades from Grade 1—6. I was in Grade 6, Ronald in Grade 5 and Willy in Grade 3. Consequently, when I passed into Grade 7, I had to attend Lively Public School. It was a long walk, but I didn't mind at all as I was accompanied by my friends. The following year, a class picture was taken at 1-D Waters School with Creightonite teacher, Mrs. Pat Fortune. My three brothers were all present and so we have this rare photo of the three of them. Ronald was one of the older boys, Willy soon found Gary Brazier and other friends and little Franky's friend was Alan Liscum. Franky, in Grade One, was not yet wearing glasses then.

My brother Willy was killed by a drunk driver in March of 1960, almost in front of our home. We could no longer stay there. Willy was 15 years old. My parents were devastated! The house had to be sold. The one bright spot that year was the birth of lovely baby sister Lillian, just 6 weeks after that accident. Our neighbours, Alan and Patricia Green, purchased the house. Too many sad memories lingered there for our family.

MEMBERS OF THE "21 CLUB":

ALICE de BURGER in front;

(Second row) THERESA McPARLAND, KARIN MAKELA, GERRY WILSON , ROSA KOWALENKO,

(last row) ELSA SEYWERD, MABLE QUIRING, ETHEL LISCUM, BEA NICHOLSON

OLIVE SNELL, ENID GOODWARD, ALMA BRAZIER,

MARGARET DAWSON, BERTHA GARDNER, HILMA ANDERSON, MARGE EVANS

Ladies of the "21 Club"

Erna, Verna Spencer, Barbara Green, Lorraine Mead — my friends.

MARYMOUNT PIONEER

IN 1957, IT was time to choose a high school. I was 16. I had heard of this new school for Catholic girls from our Parish Priest. It was called Marymount College and located in Sudbury. I knew that buses would take me there as well as boys to St. Charles College. I was excited to begin my new educational experience. I had no idea of what an adventure it would turn out to be! It was September of 1957.

When the bus arrived at the school, we discovered that the school's construction had not been completed. We were directed where to go and began our climb to the top storey of what later became the Convent of the Sisters of St. Joseph. We were the first Marymount students. Because of this, only Grade 9 was offered. There were three classes of 30 students in each class. Sisters of St. Joseph taught us. I remember that Sister Estelle was principal, Sister Alicia taught Science and Math and there was one other teacher who I believe was Miss Mc Donald who taught English. My memory may be erroneous on this point as it was after all, more than 60 years ago.

We wore uniforms very different from those worn later. I had a grey jumper, white blouse with a little blue ribbon in the top button, a cobalt blue blazer and sturdy black oxford laced shoes with clear nylons. Silver and blue were the school's colours in those early days. I was proud of that uniform, the first uniform I ever wore.

Since there were only 90 students, we became acquainted with each other very quickly. Going up these long stairs was not something any of us had anticipated upon entering high school. Once we entered our classrooms, we noticed immediately that the construction of these rooms had not been accomplished either. As a result, electricians on ladders were working above our heads. It happened that I knew one of these electrical workers as he was Dutch, as I was. (The Dutch community was very small in the Sudbury area at the time.) He would smile at me at times which was a distraction I must admit. Plumbers were doing their work outside the classrooms. We encountered tradesmen of all kinds trying to finish their assigned jobs everywhere.

The desks had been set up in each room as well as a teacher's desk and some blackboards. The instruction by the teachers under these extreme conditions was nevertheless excellent. We learned a school song as well as the motto, "Disce ut Vivas" which meant "Learn to Live" appropriately. I still remember bits of the school song which went, "Disce ut Vivas let us sing; to Alma Mater honour bring. We promise loyalty to you, beneath the silver and the blue".

I don't know whether that still is the Marymount school song or even the motto but those words have stuck in my mind all these years, so they were meaningful to me obviously.

Erna in Marymount uniform 1957

MY FIRST JOB

ON JUNE 7, 1957, I had turned 16 and I wanted to work for the summer. The Massey Family of Creighton Mine owned a tourist lodge named Pine Cove Lodge, at Wolseley Bay of French River. My mother had heard that Mrs. Massey preferred to hire local staff. She convinced me to call her and Eileen Massey hired me immediately. Mr. Archie Massey picked me up in his truck two days later and I began to work that very weekend. Little did I realize what was in store for me.

Being a kitchen helper entailed washing dishes for a staff of thirty and the dining room guests which numbered up to 102 at capacity. Two of us were assigned to this monumental task. We all worked seven days a week as we lived on the premises and slept in a sort of barrack which also housed many mice. I hated them. Our pay as kitchen helpers was the magnificent sum of $50 a month! There were no days off from the July 1st weekend until the end of the Labour Day weekend as school started the next day.

Another facet of our job was to assist the two cooks. One was the pastry cook and the other prepared the entrees. Mary Ostashek, the entrée cook, had a specialty which she prepared every Sunday morning. It was borscht soup—Ukrainian beet soup. We kitchen girls had to clean mountains of beets, carrots and potatoes every Saturday evening. Our fingers and hands became raw and sore and stained red and orange by the vegetables we came to hate! We tried bleach which was damaging to our skin but we had to do something. Coating our hands at night with Vaseline remedied the condition somewhat.

About fifteen teenagers worked at Pine Cove Lodge which was a fishing lodge for tourists. Every morning the boys ensured that the boats were ready before 7 am with fishing gear, motors filled with gasoline, floatation cushions, and the necessary ingredients for the shore lunch which the Indigenous guides prepared for the guests. The guys slept in the boat-house on the other side of the bridge which connected the main lodge to where the cabins were located.

Pine Cove consisted of 40 cabins, the large lodge and bar, a large laundry, the dining room, kitchen, and tuck shop. They were all built of large logs, the trim being white and red. Set among the tall majestic pine trees, the cabins were a lovely contrast. Some of the cabins were designated as "housekeeping" so the tourists who rented these did their own cooking, cleaning, and made their own beds with linen provided by Pine Cove. Usually these tourists stayed for extended periods of time, as long as six weeks in the case of the McBurney's from London, Ontario, whom I came to know well.

We worked hard with little time off but we also had a lot of fun enjoying campfires on the beach in the evenings, swimming, sing-alongs around the piano in the lodge with pianist Carolyn Ostashek, dancing to the latest hits on the jukebox, playing tricks on each other in our sleep quarters etc., all of which alleviated the stress of work.

We were allowed to swim and use the canoes during our time off and for me this experience meant learning new skills as well as developing a love affair with the beautiful French River.

On Thursday evenings, all of us went to the dance at Wolseley Lodge a 15-minute boat ride down the bay. A country and western band played music and it was the high point of our week. We danced with the guys we worked with, as well as the guests from our lodge. Strong friendships were forged during this first summer and the next three summers that I worked there and many have lasted until today.

In the fifties, the guests were nearly all Americans and their licence plates indicated Ohio, Pennsylvania, New York and Michigan. Often the tourists came in groups of four or six men all avid fishermen. A carload of male high school graduates arrived one Sunday that first year. They generated a lot of interest among the young female staffers. I fell in love for the first time that summer with a 17 year—old young man named Chris Catanese from Cleveland, Ohio. This trip to Canada was a graduation present from his parents. The guys were surprised to discover there were many teenage girls working there—an unexpected bonus. Chris and I felt a mutual attraction at once. He returned to see me later in the summer. It was exciting and wonderful! We parted sadly and promised to write to one another during the winter. Chris invited me to come to Cleveland for American Thanksgiving in November but I had to refuse reluctantly, knowing well that my parents would never allow that.

In September, it was back to school with my wondrous secret—I was in love! I eagerly awaited his letters and when they arrived, I rushed up to my bedroom to read them in delicious privacy. Slowly they were becoming fewer and the tone was changing. Finally, in November I received a very thick letter from Chris. I flew up the stairs to my bedroom with my long - awaited treasure. As I began to read it, my heart broke. I could not believe what I was reading. "Erna, it must have been the beautiful pine trees and your amazing Canadian skies but it's Pat I love. Erna, I hope you can forgive me."

I was devastated! The acute pain I experienced dictated that I would never allow myself to care so deeply about anyone I met in the summer. It was an unexpected lesson that I learned that first year of working at Pine Cove.

Pine Cove Lodge

That painful lesson lasted until August 2, 1959. As I was going down for breakfast at 6 am, I noticed three young guys washing their faces at the end of the dock. Curious, I approached them to ask who they were and where they had come from. They had slept in their car near Pine Cove Lodge. The guys were all from Sudbury and had come to see Marilyn, the girlfriend of one of them named Alex. She worked at Waverly Lodge next to the Lodge where I worked. However, they discovered she was wearing an identification bracelet which said "Freddy" not Alex. That was the end of that relationship. The teens asked if they could hang around until the afternoon when I had finished working. Alex asked if he me could return later in the week to see me. I told him of the Thursday night dances at Wolseley Bay but that we were expected to dance with Pine Cove's guests. I had not forgotten the heartache from the summer of 1957. However, that curly hair, those brown eyes, ...and the rest is history as they say. We were married in December 1963.

MY BROTHER WILLY
1944–1960

THE WAR WAS nearly over in the southern province of Zeeland in The Netherlands where we lived. Hospital beds had been reserved for wounded soldiers until now. However, a bed was found for my mother to give birth, and on June 18, 1944, my brother Willy was born. He was the third child and second son of my parents. (I was the first—born but I was a girl). Willy was left-handed like our Dad. The Brothers at his school rapped him sharply on the hand in Grade One each time he tried to use it. Our mother went to the school and firmly put a stop to that.

Willy was seven years old when we immigrated to Canada in 1951. He was much relieved that using his left hand was acceptable here. So was Mom. Willy loved to go into the bush to hike, fish and just spend time there. He always told Mom where he was going and when he planned to be home. Joining the Boy Scouts was natural for Willy where he learned many abilities such as using a compass, tying knots, building a campfire and other skills as well. He loved every minute he spent as a Scout.

March 12, was a warm spring day so Dad took down the bikes in the garage. He repaired the spokes, oiled the chains, getting them ready for spring time. In the evening, my boyfriend Alex and I were at my friend's house waiting for Lorraine's boyfriend to come and take us all to see a movie in Sudbury. Willy had attended the 14th birthday party of his friend Jack Walton in the afternoon, we learned later.

Suddenly, we noticed that there was a great commotion on the road in front of her house. Alex and Lorraine went to see what was happening. As soon as Alex saw Willy, he identified him. Then he ran back to get me, "Erna, it's Willy, we have to go to tell your parents!" My brother had been hit by a car? He was watching TV when we left 15 minutes earlier. So many questions!! Why was he on the road? Such deep fears!

By this time someone had already told my Dad. When the ambulance arrived, my father climbed in the back with Willy, going to Memorial Hospital in Sudbury. Surgery was performed immediately, to no avail. Dad phoned home for someone to bring Mom to the hospital right away. A neighbour, Maria Bruyns, a nurse, drove her there. It was too late. She called our home from the hospital and asked to speak to my boyfriend Alex. I told her to tell me what I had already guessed, that my brother was dead. He had died at 10:15 pm. The driver of the car came to our house that night to say that he was sorry. I did not realise that's who he was. We were told much later that he had been drinking at the Lively Legion that afternoon. Much later in court, he was assessed 60% of the blame for the accident and Willy 40%.

Our house was full of supportive neighbours by this time and they understood immediately that Willy had passed away. When my parents arrived home, they were speechless in their grief. Dad took Mom upstairs to bed right away. Our mother was eight months pregnant and he feared that this enormous shock might affect her or the baby.

Sunday morning at Mass at St. Michael's in Creighton Mine, Father Regan announced to the parishioners what had occurred in our family. Creightonites sprang into action to assist us in any way possible. Food arrived all day.

After Mass on Sunday, someone told us that Willy had been riding his bike when he was hit. This news shocked all of us and didn't make sense. Willy, who had always been so responsible, so cautious, was riding a bike, at night? The crushed bicycle was brought to our house from a neighbour's backyard. All of us were very upset to see it. My brother Ron quickly dragged it into the garage out of my Mother's sight.

At Lougheed's Funeral Home on Eyre St. numerous people came to show support on Sunday and Monday. Our neighbours, classmates, teachers, and even strangers consoled us and prayed with us the whole time.

Willy's funeral took place in the packed St. Michael's Church at 9 am on Tuesday with Father Regan officiating. The First Waters Boy Scouts formed an honour guard on the church steps. The pall bearers were classmates from St. Charles College brought to Creighton Mine by bus. Willy was buried in the Lasalle Catholic Cemetery. He would have turned 16 in June.

When I was cleaning and sorting some family papers in 2015, I found Willy's "Book of Remembrance!" I had been wondering what had happened to it and here I had it all along. l was shocked and tears sprang into my eyes. It listed his pall bearers, people who came to support our family, classmates and teachers of all of us. The pall bearers were Jack Walton, Frank Falzetta, Wayne Loupelle, Alvin Sokoloski, Marc Roy, Bob Moyle. Many Creightonites, people from Dogpatch, a number of priests and Sisters, Scouts, his classmates, many Dutch people attended his funeral. It was literally an outpouring of condolences and love. We had been in Canada nine years at this time and we had no relatives in this country, but we learned that the kind support of friends was a source of deep consolation.

PHOTOS WITH WILLY

Collage with brothers, sisters and his friends. Below, his First Communion, Hulst,1951

Below: Willy's First Communion in Hulst.

CANADIANS

OUR FAMILY HAD been in Canada for 10 years in 1961. We were still mourning the death of our 15-year-old brother Willy and rejoicing in the birth of our baby sister Lillian. My brother Ron and I approached our father about applying for Canadian citizenship. He was so deep in his grief that he had not given it any thought and we understood that. He agreed and since neither Ron nor I were 21 yet he had to apply for us and our younger brother Franky named Franciscus on the form. Ron and I got information as to what agency to apply to. It was the Department of Citizenship and Immigration at that time. Consequently, on May 30, 1961 the Treasury Office sent our father an official receipt for $7.00, the cost of the application. A small sum for such an important request even for 1961.

On September 6, Dad received a receipt for $20 for "Petitions for Canadian Citizenship" for him, my mother and the three of his children named, Erna Johanna Maria, Ronald Joseph and Franciscus Louisa de Burger. And thus, we became citizens of this wonderful country, Canada. I vaguely remember visiting the Court House in Sudbury for the "Court of Canadian Citizenship". There certainly was no celebration of any kind for us there. I don't remember having to answer any history questions.

When I went to Teachers' College in North Bay in September of 1961, at one point when one of my professors said something about a good Canadian girl could endure the cold, I told him I was Dutch. That necessitated a visit to the office of the principal, Mr. Dyell. I explained that we had just received Canadian citizenship a month before and I was not used to identifying myself as Canadian yet. Of course, that changed over the years and I now know that I am indeed Canadian and am very proud of it!

The de Burger Family today has members who have Franco-Canadian, Ukrainian, Finnish, Belgian, Scottish, Italian, and other nationalities' members backgrounds like so many other Canadian families. That makes our family truly Canadian! We are proud of each and every one and treasure them all. The family is four generations deep in this phenomenal land.

Five family members are buried in Canadian soil. We love and honour the Canadian flag and vote in every election. My parents probably had to swear an oath and answer questions about Canada at the Citizen's Court but I don't really recall that. In any case we were now full Canadian citizens forever with all the rights and obligations that entails. Canada is our country and always will be.

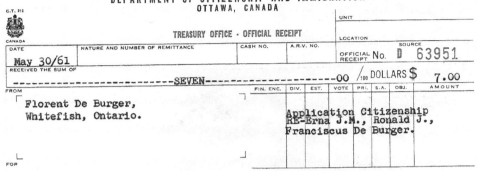

DEPARTMENT OF CITIZENSHIP AND IMMIGRATION
OTTAWA, CANADA

C.T. 312

CANADA

TREASURY OFFICE - OFFICIAL RECEIPT

UNIT	
LOCATION	

DATE	NATURE AND NUMBER OF REMITTANCE	CASH NO.	A.R.V. NO.	OFFICIAL RECEIPT No.	SOURCE D 63951
May 30/61					

RECEIVED THE SUM OF

-----------------------------------SEVEN-----------------------------00 /100 DOLLARS $ 7.00

FROM

Florent De Burger,
Whitefish, Ontario.

FIN. ENC.	DIV.	EST.	VOTE	PRI.	S.A.	OBJ.	AMOUNT

Application Citizenship
RE-Erna J.M., Ronald J.,
Franciscus De Burger.

FOR

AUTHORIZED SIGNING OFFICER

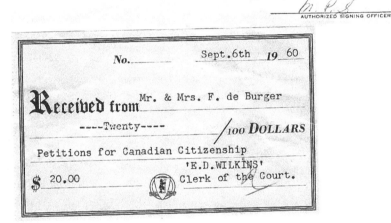

No.___   Sept.6th 19 60

Received from Mr. & Mrs. F. de Burger

----Twenty----   /100 **DOLLARS**

Petitions for Canadian Citizenship

'E.D.WILKINS'

$ 20.00   Clerk of the Court.

		RECEIVED FROM / REÇU DE	5 (T)	5 (1)	5 (2)A	5 (2)A	5 (2)B	5 (2)B	4 (3)	3 +18	3 −18	3		8	10	26B VI	AMOUNT RECEIVED
CR COURT BUREAU	88 NOV 01 DATE	DeBurger Mr Florent SURNAME/NOM GIVEN NAMES/PRÉNOMS	40	—	25	—	40	25	0	20	5	—	(88.)			0	20 — MONTANT REÇU

Secretary Secrétariat
of State d'État

OFFICIAL RECEIPT
REÇU OFFICIEL   918905

COURT OF CANADIAN CITIZENSHIP
BUREAU DE LA CITOYENNETE CANADIENNE

PLEASE PRESENT THIS RECEIPT OR REFER TO THIS
NUMBER IF YOU HAVE ANY FURTHER ENQUIRY.

SI VOUS DÉSIREZ DE PLUS AMPLES RENSEIGNE-
MENTS, VEUILLEZ PRÉSENTER CE REÇU OU MEN-
TIONNER CE NUMÉRO.

ISSUED BY
EMIS PAR

SIGNATURE

NOTE: THE APPLICATION(S) FEE(S) IS NOT REFUNDABLE
NOTE: LES DROITS À ACQUITTER POUR DÉPOSER UNE
DEMANDE NE SONT PAS REMBOURSABLES

SEC 3-68 (11/80)

Citizenship documents

BECOMING A TEACHER

WAS I A "born teacher" as my mother used to say—I'm not sure. I do know that from my earliest memories I loved "playing school" with my dolls and a blackboard on a stand-up easel that I had received on St. Nicholas Day—December 6, while a child in Holland. I loved explaining things to children younger than me and convinced them to play school with me whenever I could. Since I had three younger brothers, this was not always an easy task as they preferred active games. My love of reading fit right in with school—type activities.

We came to Canada when I was 10 years old so there was a steep learning curve as I had to learn to read and write in English. I seemed to have an affinity for the language and was soon enjoying library books in my new language. When I was 11, we moved to Creighton Mine and I attended Creighton Mine Public School where I was placed in Grade 5. My teacher took an interest in me and I truly believe that fact lit the desire in me to become a teacher.

Success at school in elementary and high school convinced me that becoming a teacher was the career for me. Accordingly, after graduating from Grade 13 at Copper Cliff High School in June of 1961, off I went to North Bay Teachers' College. I loved every day of that one—year course especially being in the classroom and finally getting the opportunity to actually teach! Some people complained about some of the tedious things we had to do, but not me. I knew that learning to print and write properly, was necessary in order for me to be able to teach the children.

Learning how to teach reading and phonics was a revelation to me as I learned many nuances of the language that I had used but not understood. The college library became my second home. I needed to know the literature which was suitable and of interest to the various grade levels. Besides that, reading for pleasure was my relaxation when my work was done. It still is! During my practice teaching assignments in and around North Bay as well as in Sudbury, contact with the pupils excited me. I remember being sent to Cobalt for one week in February of 1962 along with two classmates. It was extremely cold and the snow banks were nearly as high as the homes. The billeting family which hosted us was very kind and treated us well. The lady was an excellent cook who spoiled us with the best of home cooking. The pupils were respectful and the practice teacher helpful. My evaluation at the end of that week was very good. Later that year I was assigned a week at Naughton Public School in a Grade 7. One of the lessons I was asked to teach, was a math lesson helping students to understand the difference between a bill and a receipt. One boy was experiencing difficulty understanding the concept. However, by the end of my lesson, I saw the proverbial light bulb go on indicating that he understood my explanations. What a thrill for me!

In April, there was a job fair at the college. Representatives of school boards came from across the province to recruit teachers for their staffs. There were over 500 of us graduating in 1962 and we had our choice of where we wanted to begin our careers. Mr. Gordon Whalen, the principal of Creighton Mine Public School and his secretary Irene Simpson, interviewed and hired me that day. He had taught me at Lively Public school in Grade 7 so we were already acquainted. I was so excited now that I actually knew where I would be teaching! He also hired two of my classmates, -Barbara Fraser and Helen Hughes. He told me that I would have a grade 3 or 4. It didn't matter to me—I would love it, I knew that.

The graduation dance in May was a wonderful evening of accomplishment and anticipation. My boyfriend Alex came from Sudbury for it! Now it was official—I was a certified teacher in the Province of Ontario!

Shortly after I arrived home at my parents' home in Whitefish at the end of May, the phone rang. It was for me! The teacher in the one - room school at Worthington needed to take time off as his daughter had been seriously injured in a car accident in North Bay—could I come to take his place until he returned? Talk about baptism by fire! When I arrived at the school whether it was my youth or the fact that they loved their teacher, I wasn't sure, but the pupils did not accept me. They did all they could to disrupt my lessons and challenged my authority in every way! I was shocked that the children would show such disrespect to me and I was unsure of what to do. However, it was my responsibility to teach these children to the best of my ability and that is what I was determined to do. After a few very long days things were going smoothly. My self - confidence was restored.

I moved into the Teachers' Residence on Snider St. in Creighton Mine at the end of August and began my preparations immediately for my first official day of teaching the Grade 3 /4 class which was now mine. Preparing lessons, decorating the bulletin boards, arranging the furniture, becoming acquainted with the other staff members, were all tasks which I enjoyed immensely! The first day of school finally arrived and as I was walking to Creighton Mine Public School. I was excited but also somewhat fearful as I wondered if I would be able to teach these eight -and nine -year- olds. The fact that I had been a pupil at this school when I was a child, added to my sense of eagerness. It was a very emotional day for me!

Barbara Fraser, Helen Hughes and I often returned to the school after dinner to prepare for the next day. This did not feel like a burden but that it was exactly what we needed to do for our pupils. I recall arriving back at the Residence well after 10 pm from school on more than one occasion. One of my pupils was diagnosed with rheumatic fever that first year so I went to her home which was close to the Residence, and taught her there so that she would not lag behind her classmates. She returned to school for the months of May and June and achieved over 80% in her final Grade 4 exams. I was so very proud of Kathy! The Creighton parents were most supportive and the children very respectful which made teaching joyful and productive.

The second year that I was teaching was a most eventful year as Alex and I had decided to get married on December 28, 1963. 1963 was the year that President John Kennedy was assassinated in the U.S. on November 22. Our principal, Gordon Whalen, knocked on each of our doors and told the teachers what had transpired. Then he opened the PA system to all our classrooms so that we could hear the radio reports as they were being broadcast. It was most frightening as we had no idea where this horrific event might lead. The Solar System, the subject of my lesson at the time, was soon forgotten. I also felt the responsibility to keep my students as calm as possible which meant having to hide my own emotions.

When I arrived at my parents' home in Whitefish, the television was already on—most unusual. The next day we watched in horror as Jack Ruby shot Lee Harvey Oswald—on live TV! That entire weekend we were all glued to our TV watching events unfold after this unbelievable assassination of the young American president, just 44 years old. Mrs. Jacqueline Kennedy evidenced amazing poise as she stood and watched the caisson with her husband's body go by, while holding the hands of her two young children. I will never forget that terrible weekend!

On my wedding day, I welcomed at least a dozen of my pupils to the reception in Creighton Mine at Cabrini Hall next to the Catholic Church. Their mothers had called to ask if the children were indeed invited. I replied definitely as they were a very important part of my life. The little girls loved to see their teacher as a bride! I told the children that my name was Mrs. Fex, would they remember that? They assured me that they would.

My husband and I moved into Carbone's Apartments right across the street from the school. My pupils tried very hard to remember my new name but if they failed, they had to put a penny into the Red Cross jar. Every Friday afternoon we had a Red Cross program consisting of skits and songs and discussing the admirable work of that organization wherever there was a need. Both the children and I looked forward to these afternoons. It was a more relaxed hour and gave me the opportunity to learn about my students' talents and interests - important in getting to know the whole child.

I became pregnant for our first child shortly in the Spring. In the sixties once a teacher became pregnant, she had to resign as soon as she started to "show"'. Accordingly, in June of 1964, I was required to submit my letter of resignation to the Creighton Mine Public School Board. I did so reluctantly.

My healthy baby girl was born in November 1964. We named her Jacqueline, after Jacqueline Kennedy who I had admired so much for her bravery. Unexpectedly, in January of 1965, Mr. George Stephens, the new principal, called me to ask if I would return to teach his Grade 8 class as "Principal's Relief". I would be teaching the English program three afternoons a week. Since my neighbour Irene Gignac offered to take care of Jacqueline for me, I agreed readily. It felt good to return to teaching even if it was part time. This meant that while most of my time was spent happily with my new baby, I was also able to return to teach. I liked being part of the staff again!

Unfortunately, my teaching career ended on a negative note when at the last school I taught, a Grade 8 student threatened to kill me and in her words, "Throw my body parts all over my yard". She actually uttered such a death threat to me. I was shaking and ran to the principal's office who phoned the girl's mother immediately. The mother arrived at the school very quickly and to her credit insisted we call the police. The officer came to the school in his cruiser. He interviewed both the student and myself after which he asked me if I wished to lay charges against her. I said no. I knew her troubled background and was hesitant to add to that. However, if I had charged her, she would have understood the severity of threatening death to someone.

To tell the truth, at home later I was angry that my career which I had loved so much should end this way. Of course, after some time I got over that and chose to remember all the wondrous aspects of teaching, through the years. I retired in 1996.

Living in Sudbury which is close by to where I have taught, I often run into my former students. They often introduce me to their grandchildren with a warm, deferential, "This is Mrs. Fex". I really enjoy seeing them again and hearing how well that they have done in their life.

Creighton Mine Public School - Print

Erna at Teacher's Desk

Life at the Residence

I LOVED LIVING at the Teacher's Residence - it was such fun!

When Mr. Gordon Whalen, principal, hired me to teach at Creighton Mine Public School in May of 1962, I discovered that I could rent a room at the Teachers' Residence. It was inexpensive for room and board, and since it was only a 10-minute walk to school, it was ideal.

This was not the first Teachers' Residence in Creighton Mine. That was constructed in 1922 and located on Lake Street. The Teachers' Residence at 20 Snider Street, was built in 1916 as a boarding house and clubhouse for the mine's engineers. In 1944, it officially became the Teachers' Residence. There were two bedrooms on the main floor as well as a large living room with a stone fireplace, formal dining room, kitchen, bathroom and an apartment for the housekeeper. On the second floor were five bedrooms and a bathroom.

Life at the residence was most enjoyable. The only drawback was how cold the bedrooms were in winter. I wore white socks to bed every night. We were fortunate to have a housekeeper so we never had to cook or clean. I had never experienced such luxury and found it quite easy to get used to! Living with the other teachers facilitated becoming well acquainted with each other. Beginning teachers were Helen Hughes, Barbara Fraser and me. The others, Eileen Mulligan, Muriel Bertrand, Jim Kaay, Hugh Imerson, Lois Cramm, were all well—experienced and they were generous in sharing their expertise with us as were Mrs. Rita Craigen,

Mrs. Saimi Seppala, Mrs. Verna Gutsch, principal Gordon Whalen and secretary Irene Simpson. Provided with excellent meals and only having responsibilities for our own bedrooms, allowed us to concentrate on school. I became immersed in my schoolwork, loving every minute of it!

We enjoyed many parties at the residence. Hallowe'en, Christmas, other occasions had to be celebrated! We shared family events, such as when my father suffered a heart attack underground in the mine in 1962. My colleagues were supportive and reassuring. I really appreciated that as I was very worried.

On December 28, 1963, unbelievably, three of us on staff were married on the same day. Jim Kaay married Maureen in Barry's Bay, Muriel Bertrand married Creightonite Marty McAllister, and I married Sudburian Alex Fex. Our reception was at Cabrini Hall located adjacent to St. Michael's Catholic Church in Creighton Mine. Parish priest Father Regan was able to attend which pleased me immensely. He was so kind to our family from the first time we attended Mass at St. Michael's. Whitefish parish was now my parents' parish, and their priest, Father Joseph Hompes, attended the reception as well. Ten of my pupils came to see me in my bridal finery. I was as pleased to see them as they were excited. Even my parents enjoyed seeing the children at the reception.

Creighton kids loved to come to the Residence to show us their costumes and collect candy on Hallowe'en night. I'm sure nearly every child in town made it to our door! We loved trying to guess who they were. Sometimes a high school student would knock on the door of the residence seeking help in a difficult subject. They had such a comfort level with their former teachers. One young man, Doug Porteous, came seeking assistance in grade 9 math and I was pleased to assist him on several nights until I was sure he had grasped the concepts. He reminded me and thanked me many years later.

Life at the Teachers' Residence was comfortable and congenial. The social occasions were delightful, stimulating and just plain fun! Many of us became life—long friends. The memories I have of living there are precious!

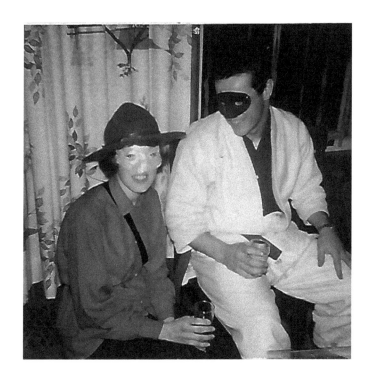

Alex & Erna—Hallowe'en party at the residence

My Father's Heart Attack (1962)

CHRISTMAS 1962 WAS a happy day for all of us at my parents' home in Whitefish. The store was closed of course, giving Mom and Dad a well—deserved day off. The following day was Boxing Day another day of rest for all of us, that is, except my Dad who was working at #9 shaft in Creighton Mine. Alex and I were visiting my mother and siblings and enjoying each other's company.

It was about 7 o'clock when the phone rang in the store—the only phone they had in the building. Mom went to answer it returning to the living room as very pale with tears in her eyes. "Your father has suffered a heart attack in the mine. That was Dr. McGruther calling. He's sending your Dad to the Copper Cliff Hospital. We can go to see him tomorrow." What a shock to all of us! Dad was only 47 years old. The mood in the house changed immediately as we were all trying to digest this frightening news.

After diagnosing my father, the doctor sent him to the Copper Cliff Hospital but by taxi, not ambulance. When the taxi arrived at the hospital the circular drive-way was full of snow. No one had cleared it. The cab driver said to my Dad, "Can you get in there by yourself?" My father was a proud man and agreed that he was capable of doing so. Dad got out of the taxi and with great difficulty waded through the deep snow. As he opened the door to the hospital, a nurse came towards him to ask his name. He told her and that Dr. McGruther had sent him here from Creighton Mines because he had suffered a heart attack. Immediately they put him on a gurney, undressed him, took his blood pressure, and told him firmly that he was not to shave, wash or get out of bed. This was after he had floundered through those very deep snow drifts!

He spent six weeks in Copper Cliff Hospital and received excellent care. He couldn't praise the staff enough. We were grateful for that! Dr. Stanyon was Dad's cardiologist. While asking the usual questions about his previous health status, he asked him if he smoked. Dad admitted that he smoked about 2 packs per day and worked underground at Creighton Mine. The doctor then asked my father his age. Dad replied "47" where upon the cardiologist asked him bluntly, "Do you want to reach 48?" Of course, he said yes. "Then quit smoking!" To his credit my father never smoked again. That frightening brush with his mortality convinced him.

When he was finally discharged from the hospital to go home, he and my mother changed their lifestyles even their diet. When he was strong enough, he bought a second-hand bicycle and rode it as often as weather and his strength allowed it. When winter arrived, he purchased a stationary bike which he placed in his bedroom and he exercised on it for at least 30 minutes every day. He was off work for 7 months. When he returned, he was given a job on surface—light duty they called it at INCO.

My father's heart attack changed the whole family's life as we were made aware of the dangers of smoking and the importance of exercise. He maintained this new lifestyle and lived to be nearly 92 years old. What no one in our family expected, not even him, was that he would outlive our mother by 10 years! Dad died June 15, 2007, Father's Day weekend, of heart disease.

Dad (Florent on stationary bike)

The Dutchies Are Coming

OUR ENTIRE FAMILY was so excited! Our maternal grandparents were coming to visit us in Canada in 1962. We had not seen them since we had immigrated in 1951. My mother was especially thrilled as she had always been very close to her parents whom we called Mit (grandmother) and Pit (grandfather).

I keenly missed having relatives in Canada as we had visited our maternal grandparents most Sundays and our paternal grandmother very often as well.

My grandparents, aunts, uncles, cousins—lived in close proximity to one another and to us in The Netherlands. Even my great- grandmother whom we called Opoe, lived nearby. In Canada, when I would hear the kids at school speak of visiting their grandparents, I felt very lonely. But now our own grandparents were coming for a two-month visit!

Mit and Pit were flying for the first time in their lives. The Dutch government had organized and subsidized this trip for parents of Dutch family members who had immigrated. The day they were to arrive, our entire family as well as our Dutch parish priest, Father Joseph Hompes, drove to Malton Airport in Toronto. The joy was palpable among those waiting! I remember that one lady knocked on a window so hard that it broke when she spied her mother! My grandmother recorded that incident in her journal. When we spotted our grandparents, we all waved to them excitedly. Big smiles were on their faces too. The Customs officers checked these people's paper work expeditiously. In fact, these officers were smiling and kind to these elderly people. Then we were hugging and kissing our amazing family members. I happily presented my grandmother with a large bouquet of carnations. My grandparents found the drive from Toronto to Sudbury endless. The distances in Canada cannot be compared to the concept of distances in The Netherlands. They were very tired after their long flight.

Both of our grandparents were happy to help out in any way they could. My grandmother helped with the ironing and other household chores. My grandfather planted a number of poplar trees in front of the church we attended, St. Christopher's Church in Whitefish. When my grandmother's hair needed to be washed and curled, I was happy to do that for her. During their stay when she needed a cut, Mom made an appointment with Creighton Mine's talented hairdresser Sophie, who also permed my grandmother's hair before her journey back home.

My grandfather loved to fish and went often with my brothers Ronald and Franky to the nearby Vermillion River. Frequently, they were successful and came home proudly with a number of fish. My mother always prepared the delicious fresh fish for lunch that day.

Reading my grandmother's journal is very interesting. So many memories came flooding back of that auspicious summer of 1962. The journal came into my possession recently and is a veritable treasure to me. Of course, I knew about it but I had no idea that it had been given to my mother. My sister Lillian happened to discover it in a cardboard box and presented it to me at a recent Family Reunion in Barrie. So many memories came flooding back of that special summer of 1962. When they arrived home, in Sint Jansteen, The Netherlands, all their grandchildren (except the 5 of us) awaited them. Someone had made a large, lovely banner saying, "Welkom thuis", welcome home. Their arrival at home was celebrated by all family members present.

Arrival – with Erna

Leaving home

Group-de Burgers; Grandparents

Ready to return home

Arrival at home – family waiting

Collage of pictures

Our Wedding

ALTHOUGH WE HAD been dating for more than four years, it was still a lovely surprise when Alex proposed to me in September of 1963. There was no doubt in my mind that I wanted to marry him. We were in my parents' home in Whitefish when he asked me that momentous question. Of course, I said, "YES!" My mother and father came out of the store after having served their customers, and we immediately gave them our exciting news. They congratulated us and asked when we planned to be married. It was then that Alex asked my father for my hand.

A spring wedding had always appealed to me so we decided that Easter weekend would be a good time. This would give us enough time to plan our wedding as I was teaching at Creighton Mine Public School and wanted to save money for the thrilling day. My parents explained that we would be expected to pay for our own wedding as my father had been off work with pneumonia for quite some time.

As fall began, Alex and I asked ourselves why we were waiting until spring since we knew each other so well and had no doubts that we were meant for each other. As a result, we moved our wedding date up to December 28 instead. My mother was not amused! This meant that not only did she need to prepare for Christmas but also for her eldest daughter's wedding just after Christmas! Another problem for my parents was that they had no idea what needed to be done for a wedding in Canada, as it was quite different from a wedding in Holland. That left all of the decision—making up to Alex and me.

Alex had contacted his best friend, Dennis Taus, to ask him to be his best man. Dennis, however, was serving with the United Nations' Peacekeeping Force in Cyprus and was unable to get leave to come home in December. He was very disappointed as we were. To make up for his absence, Dennis sent me 12 metres of the most beautiful shimmering Egyptian brocade and asked if I would consider having my wedding gown made of this material. I was overwhelmed and of course agreed and told him so in a letter immediately. I approached Mrs. Mary Ostashek and asked her if she would have time to accomplish this before Christmas. Together we chose a pattern, which would display this amazing material to its best advantage and decided something simple and elegant was what was needed. I was living at the Teachers' Residence in Creighton at the time and Mary lived on Alexander Street not far from there so fittings were not a problem after school. Mrs. Ostashek, an experienced seamstress, constructed my beautiful gown and since I had plenty of material, she suggested a long self-lined train which had a wide sash that could be removed for dancing at the reception. Alex planned to rent a tuxedo for our wedding, which cost the huge sum of $ 12. at the time.

However now we had a problem in that Alex had to find a new "best man" to be a witness at our wedding. He asked my brother Ron who consented at once. We had planned on having Ron in the wedding party in any case so he just moved up to a more important position. Alex then asked his good friend and Spartan football buddy Ron Hewitt to be his groomsman. My close friend Sharon Heaphy had agreed to be my "maid of honour" and Alex's sister Denise Fex was my other bridesmaid. My little sisters Liesje and Lillian were junior bridesmaid and flower girl respectively. The bridesmaids and little girls all wore short dresses in a French blue colour with wedding band headpieces. The wedding party was complete. My brother Franky served as altar boy and so my whole family was involved in our wedding.

Then came the serious planning. I approached the ladies of the St. Michael's CWL in Creighton to ask if they would cater our dinner. There was some initial hesitation due to the busy Christmas season but they agreed to do so. Thank heavens! Cabrini Hall was reserved for our big day, as I wanted my pupils to be able to come to see their teacher in her wedding gown. Flowers were the next item to be decided. I had always known that I wanted my wedding bouquet to be red and white and so ordered red roses and white carnations. The bridesmaids' bouquets were pink and white. Corsages for Alex, the groomsmen, my mom and dad, Alex's mom, so much to think about!

Alex and I went to Wolfe's Book and Printing store on Durham Street in Sudbury to choose and order our invitations. When we had completed our arrangements, Mr. Wolfe presented me with a wedding gift, "The Joy of Cooking". The price was marked inside the cover - $ 7.95 Needless to say we were very pleased with this courtesy gift. I suspect that Alex was even more excited than I was since he had an expectation of the wonderful meals I would learn to cook from this book.

On November 22, we were all shocked to hear of the assassination of the youthful president of the United States, John F. Kennedy. I will never forget our principal, Mr. Gordon Whalen, coming to my classroom door to tell me of this tragedy. I remember feeling very frightened, as we did not know if this was a solitary act or if this was the beginning of a time of war. Sunday after Mass, that TV set was again turned on as we watched in horror as Jack Ruby shot Lee Harvey Oswald. We could not believe what we had just witnessed! After supper mom asked me to accompany her to the church hall for Bingo. My immediate reply was that I was watching history in the making and that I would have to teach about this some day and, "Sorry, mom, but I'm staying right here. I may be teaching about this one day." Then, Alex whispered in my ear that since we would be married soon perhaps, I should go to Bingo with my mother. I found this somewhat strange but since he kept at me, I reluctantly agreed to go. As mom, my sister Liesje and I descended the stairs leading into St. Christopher's church basement hall, people stood up and began to applaud. I then noticed Alex's mother and sisters and suddenly realized that this was a wedding shower for me. When I think back to what I put my poor mother through! Another surprise shower was held for me later at Cabrini Hall in Creighton. The parents of many of my pupils attended, as did my teaching colleagues, old neighbours, and many friends. I can't really remember how I was encouraged to go to the hall but again it was a surprise to me. I was most fortunate to receive lovely gifts in both cases.

My engagement and wedding rings, as well as Alex's wedding band were purchased at John Bazar Jewellery on Durham St. I felt so special wearing my engagement ring and glanced at it often while I was teaching and everywhere else. We had heard favourable reports of the work of photographer Tramontin whose studio was located at the top of Elm Street so made appointments for our engagement pictures as well as our wedding photos. We liked him immediately.

Next, we had to choose our wedding cake. Accordingly, we went to Cecutti's, picked out the figures for the top of the cake, and placed our order to be delivered to my parents' store in Whitefish. Another wonderful surprise—Cecutti's donated the cake as a wedding gift as my parents dealt with them on a daily basis in the store. Another one of the salesmen with whom my parents did business often, gave us two lovely Hudson Bay blankets, again totally unexpected.

One morning my mom phoned me before I went to school. That was most unusual! My father had been hospitalized at Copper Cliff Hospital with pneumonia again. He required much rest and was ordered to stay indoors for several weeks when he returned home. I was in a panic! Of course, I wanted my Dad to walk me down the aisle but the doctor had said that he must remain inside the house. I called the doctor and explained my predicament. He agreed to Dad coming to the church and reception provided he was well rested ahead of time and wore extra warm clothing. Whew! What a relief! Mom called me a second time, now just a week before our wedding. Now what? My 3-year-old sister Lillian—my flower girl, had found the scissors and cut her bangs right off. I couldn't believe it! Mom took Lillian to Sophie, the experienced Creighton hairdresser, and asked her to do what she could to salvage her haircut. Sophie's solution was to cut the hair short and comb over hair from the side to try to hide my little sister's misadventure with scissors.

On our wedding day, Saturday December 28, when Alex's brother, Leo, arrived to drive my dad and me to St. Christopher's Catholic Church, the first question I asked him was, "Is Alex at the church?" He assured me that indeed he was. Having my Dad walk me down the aisle was a deeply emotional moment for both Dad and me! However, I was going to marry the love of my life and was excited and thrilled that we would soon be man and wife. After the High Mass celebrated by

Father Joseph Hompes, we proceeded to the photographer, then to Cabrini Hall in Creighton Mine for dinner and our afternoon reception. Immediately after dinner was finished, Alex and I went outside to have our photo taken by the statue of Mary on the church lawn. It was traditional for Catholic couples in Creighton Mine to do this. Even though it was a very cold winter day, the sun was shining brightly and I would not miss out on this opportunity. About ten of my pupils came to the reception and I was as excited to see the children as they were to see me. Such fun! I informed them that my name from now on was Mrs. Fex. Could they remember that? Later we danced to music played by my brother-in-law Ron Fex and Dennis's brother Alfio Taus.

Unexpectedly, an announcement was made asking everyone to please be quiet for a few minutes for a very special reason. As this was not something Alex and I had planned we looked at each other in puzzlement. It was a phone call from my maternal grandparents in Holland! Ron Fex and Alfio had rewired the PA system so that everyone in the hall could hear the conversation. The Dutch people who were present were crying, as was I. What a wonderful emotional surprise! What a perfect gift

Then it was time to go to our apartment on George St. to get changed into our "going away" clothes. I had purchased a cranberry red three - piece suit and Alex had a new grey suit. We returned to the reception and received wonderful applause as we entered the hall. We went by train to Montreal for five days on our honeymoon and finally we had time to relax and unwind. We both fell in love with this vibrant beautiful city. An exciting new chapter of our lives had begun.

Alex & Erna Fex

Wedding party – Ron Hewitt, Denise Fex,,Liesje de Burger,,Alex & Erna Fex, Sharon Heaphy, Ron de Burger

Seated in front, Lillian de Burger.

ALWAYS A MOTHER

"A MOTHER'S LOVE is like a circle, it has no beginning and no ending". (Art Urban).

That is so true! It is also true that when a woman gives birth, she becomes a mother forever. It's certainly not something I thought about when I gave birth to my first baby Jacqueline. She was beautiful and I felt such an infusion of love immediately. I knew that I would love this child, whom I had begun to love already in utero, but was not prepared for how profound that love was! I wondered how I would feel about my second daughter, Michelle, but it was entirely the same. When my third daughter, Allison, was born my love for her was as deep as for her two sisters. It came to me then, that as a mother, my love would stretch to encompass all my children—it was automatic. And wondrous.

As my three children grew up, the deep love I had experienced at their births continued and changed imperceptibly to accommodate their choice of lifestyle. Even when their choices challenged me, my feelings toward them did not waiver.

When I was 47 years old, I became a grandmother when my daughter Michelle gave birth to her child Emily Susan. I could never have imagined that I would love this child so completely. Such strong new emotions filled me as I accepted her right away—and felt the stretch of love and tenderness for this new family member, who would be in my heart forever. Four more beautiful grandchildren followed and I love each one with unconditional love! They are so individual and each one is so fascinating in their own way.

When I phoned my parents to give them the exciting news of Emily's birth, my mother asked me to keep them informed about their first great grandchild. The baby was ill shortly after her birth. It was such a relief when she became healthy just a few days later. That's when the awareness hit me, that once a mother—always a mother even into the following generations. This enormous concept became an actuality to me when Emily, my granddaughter, gave birth to her first child—a healthy little son named Aayden. Me, a great grandmother? Even as my mother had experienced this when Emily was born, now it was me with our perfect healthy little Aayden.

Observing my daughters raising their own children was an interesting experience! Each developed their own methods, often different from mine, and all five of our grandchildren are loving, energetic and mannerly and I am so very proud of them all! Now watching my granddaughter with her little guy has brought home to me that the next generation has arrived and now I am the matriarch of this family. That fact does not make me feel old - instead I feel immensely proud of all of my descendants! Aayden's birth has made me the head of four generations of our family, even as Emily's birth caused my mother to be so. It's astonishing to experience this new facet of my life. Life is good! I am very fortunate.

With first child, Jacqueline

Published in the Inco Triangle

Our family 1988, Allison, Jacquie, Michelle

The Christening Outfit

AN HEIRLOOM—THAT'S WHAT it has become! It all happened so accidentally. Our best friend Dennis Taus had sent me beautiful brocade as a wedding gift from Egypt to be fashioned into my wedding gown.

On November 15, 1964, our first child, a daughter, whom we named Jacqueline was born to our great joy! When I phoned my close friend Sharon Heaphy to tell her our wonderful news, she asked me what had happened to the train of my wedding outfit. Sharon had been my maid of honour when we were married. I told her that it was hanging in my closet along with the gown. She immediately asked me if I would allow her to use it to make something for my new baby daughter. Sharon is a talented seamstress so I did not hesitate to agree. She called me some time later to inform me that she had completed the item, could she bring it to our home. Alex and I were absolutely thrilled when we saw what she had made. It was a christening dress and matching coat from the material of my train! Just beautiful! This was her exquisite baby gift to us.

Father Regan at St. Michael's Catholic Church in Creighton, baptized three-week-old Jacqueline on Sunday December 6, her daddy's birthday. The sun shone in through the church windows causing the lovely dress to shimmer in the light. My mother was most impressed by the talents of my former maid of honour Sharon. It was a traditional Dutch custom at that time to ask my parents to be the baby's god-parents because our child was a girl. If it had been a boy, we should have asked my husband's parents. My sister-in-law Denise was the baby's porteuse, which meant she carried the baby. That was a French tradition, which unfortunately my parents and I did not understand. My mother was upset that she was not carrying her first grandchild to the Baptismal font.

Our second daughter, Michelle, was born on June 11, 1968. Father Regan baptized her as well at St. Michael's on June 30. Her godparents were Alex's sister Lillian and her husband Guy Thibaudeau who came from Montréal for the ceremony. Naturally, our second baby wore the same christening outfit as Jacqueline had worn. Lillian commented on the elegance of the little dress and matching coat and asked where the material had originated. When I reminded her that it was from the train of my wedding gown she was most impressed.

Our third daughter Allison was born on January 16, 1974. For her baptism by Father Joseph Hompes at St. Christopher's Church in Whitefish, she also donned the lovely family baptismal ensemble even though it was a cold winter day. Allison was two weeks old and her godparents are my sister Liesje de Burger and my brother Frank de Burger.

The next child to be born in our extended family was my nephew Will de Burger. I offered our christening outfit for his baptism to his mom Shirley who accepted readily. When his sister Grace needed it, she also was gowned in it for her christening day. Since then various nieces and nephews have worn these clothes for their respective christenings. I have lent it to their Mothers happily.

Then it was the turn of the next generation. Emily, our first grandchild, was born on September 21, 1988 to our daughter Michelle and her husband Jamie McIntosh. What a thrill it was for me to see my adorable granddaughter wearing the same christening ensemble that her mother and her aunts had worn.

Next came our second granddaughter Rachel, the daughter of our eldest daughter Jacquie and her husband Scott Jordan. Rachel's birth occurred on May 17, 1995. This delightful red-haired baby was christened in St. John's Church in Toronto decked out in the by now famed baptismal garb. Her grandmother Viola Jordan loved the story of how we came to acquire this wonderful outfit. Rachel's brother Trent Jordan was born on November 21, 1997, weighing nearly 10 pounds. Our third grandchild - but our first grandson! We were most excited to meet this baby boy! When we first saw him, we wondered if he could be baptized in the traditional outfit, as he was so large for a newborn. However, our daughter assured us that he would follow the family tradition and be similarly garbed. I noticed though that the snaps at the neck could not be done up at his christening in St. John's Church.

Our next grandchild, Matthieu, was born on September 22, 2006, the son of Allison and our son-in-law Reynald Moisan. Alex and I now were the very proud grandparents of two granddaughters and two grandsons. Matthieu was baptized at St. John's in Toronto on December 17 wearing our traditional christening ensemble. Then came Matthieu's brother Nicholas in October 2008. He was baptized in Our Lady of Hope in Sudbury our church now by our parish priest Father Larry Rymes. Father Larry referred to him as Nick which surprised our daughter and son-in-law.

Aayden Alexander Robidoux, our first great-grandson—the next generation, wore the traditional Christening coat as he was 7 months old and too large to be able to wear the dress as well. To see him in the family baptismal outfit was an unimaginable thrill for Alex and me!

This wonderful Christening Outfit now hangs in my closet awaiting the next family birth. I don't allow anyone but me to wash it as it is delicate by now. I carefully launder it by hand. Unfortunately, our friend Dennis Taus has passed away so that he will never know the entire story of the amazing material and its uses through the generations and how precious it has become - albeit in a different form from what he had intended.

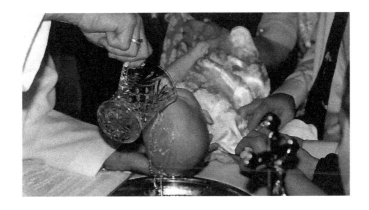

Baby Rachel being baptised

Welcome Home

IT WAS SEVERAL weeks before Christmas in 1964, and my parents asked me a big favour. They wanted to go to Holland for Christmas and New Year's. They had been longing for their families back home and wanted to spend some time enjoying this festive season with their siblings. Mom asked me if we would come to live at their house in Whitefish for the three weeks that they would be gone. This entailed taking care of her beloved canary, my brother Frank (16), my sisters Liesje (11) Lillian (4), as well as running their variety store, which was open 7 days a week.

Besides all of this, our baby Jacqueline was just six weeks old and required a lot of my attention. My husband Alex worked at Creighton Mine in the office so could only assist me afterwork and on weekends. My brother Ron was working as a health inspector in Cornwall and came home near Christmas to help as well. My parents had worked very hard in the early years in Canada and really needed a vacation. It was not easy but we made it happen for them.

On Christmas Day, my mother-in-law invited all of us for a festive turkey dinner at her home on Ontario St. in Sudbury. We really appreciated her offer and enjoyed our dinner and the company as several members of the Fex family had come home for Christmas. Some of Alex's siblings had not yet seen our baby Jacqueline so that added to the festive spirit. Naturally, we enjoyed showing her off!

My parents returned home the first week of January. In our old car we all drove to Sudbury Airport to welcome them home. My Dad's first question was, "Why didn't you come in my station wagon?" We had to tell him that Franky had an accident on Penage Rd. with that car. Dad was not happy! Mom looked at her youngest child, my sister Lillian, and immediately saw that she was covered with chicken pox. That wasn't the end of bad news for my parents. When I got up the morning of their arrival, oh no! Mom's beloved bird was laying on his back in the bird cage—dead of course. She really loved her canary. There was nothing I could do!

This was not the welcome we had wanted to give my parents but things happen, what can I say? All of these events were uncontrollable by me!

THE TELEGRAM

MY MOTHER CALLED me just before noon on February 2, 1965. From the tone of her voice I realised immediately that she was upset. Was it my Dad? She had difficulty in telling me what had happened. My father had answered the only phone which was located in their store. The call was from the CPR Telegraph office. The clerk spelled out the words with difficulty as the missive was in Dutch. My Dad eventually understood the message and relayed it to my mother, "Mother has suddenly died". Her reply, "Your mother?" his answer, "No, Alice, your mother", he told her gently. She was shocked! My parents had been in our hometown of Hulst for Christmas and New Year's and had enjoyed a wonderful vacation with their parents and siblings.

Mom had noticed that her mother was quite confused at times. She mentioned her observation to her sisters who had not noticed it at all as they saw her daily. Knowing that she was soon returning home to Canada, she called the family physician, Dr. Casparie, and expressed her concerns. He knew the family very well and had been our doctor too until we immigrated to Canada. He was alarmed when Mom said it was her mother rather than her father who needed attention. The next day he casually dropped by the house telling my grandparents that he'd love a cup of tea. Then he asked my grandfather if he could take his blood pressure. This was not unusual as the doctor had come by for an incidental visit previously. Then he suggested that since he was at their home anyway, he would take my grandmother's blood pressure as well. She refused at first but realising that she had been discovered she knew that she no longer had to cover for the fact that she had been feeling unwell and making many mental errors. After the doctor's visit she went quickly down-hill until her unexpected death on February 2 at the age of 69, of severe hardening of the arteries within her brain. Dr. Casparie had not expected that the end would come so fast.

Alex drove me from Creighton to Whitefish on his lunch hour so that I could be with my mother all afternoon. Of course, I took my baby Jacquie with me. My mother was crying when we arrived but very grateful that we had come to offer support. She was debating whether to return to The Netherlands. My parents had just returned from there four weeks previously. Her other consideration was her reluctance to travel alone to her mother's funeral. Such a dismal, lonely trip it would be. In the meantime, my head was spinning with thoughts of possibly accompanying her to Holland. My baby was very young and I could not imagine taking her with me. Who could we ask to care for her? I called my husband at work to discuss the possibility. He called his mother who agreed immediately so that important problem was solved. Secondly, I had no passport and knew that would be a major obstacle to enter Holland. I called Father Hompes who was Dutch and travelled to our homeland every year to visit his mother. He called a travel agent he knew well in North Bay and she assured him that provided we had the original telegram, that would be temporarily acceptable to go through customs in The Netherlands. So, the decision was made.

Mom and I flew from Sudbury to Montreal where we had a one- day layover, then on to Schiphol Airport in Amsterdam. My Aunt Celina and Uncle Kees met us there to take us to St. Jansteen, my mother's hometown. However, when we informed my uncle that I had no passport, he drove immediately to The Hague to the Canadian Embassy. The paper work was done applying for a passport which I would receive at my grandparent's address I was assured, and I did.

That telegram allowed me to go with my mother on this grief-stricken journey. In 1965, the telegram was the quickest way to notify family and businesses of something important and was thus a valuable document. I was grateful that it allowed me to accompany my mother for this important, tragic event in the extended family's life.

Since we arrived in Canada in 1951, I had not been able to return to Holland so I must admit I felt some excitement too. I was anxious to reconnect with my grandfather, aunts, uncles and cousins some of whom had been born after we left. I was looking forward to that as well as seeing my relatives on my Dad's side.

My grandmother's funeral was terribly sad for my grandfather. They had been married for 49 ½ years and were happily looking forward to their Golden Anniversary that coming September. It was not to be. The funeral cortege stopped in homage in front of my grandparents' store on the way to the church in Sint Jansteen. We, her family, were walking behind it and the street was lined with her neighbours and friends. My Grandmother was very popular and well-loved by her customers. During the funeral Mass, my Grandfather sobbed loudly. After the Mass we all followed the casket to the graveyard behind the church where she was laid to rest. As per Dutch custom we then walked to a nearby restaurant for koffietafel (coffee table), a reception when coffee, tea and buns with meat and cheese were provided. Then the family returned to the home of my grandparents to reminisce and socialize. It had been a gloomy but memorable day.

pic of telegram

A Cemetery Revelation

AFTER THE FUNERAL ceremonies, we stayed at my grandparents' home in Hulst for three weeks. One Sunday afternoon, my Uncle Gustaaf, invited us to go for a long drive. He was a landscaper and had to deliver some shrubs and trees to a customer near Bergen op Zoom in the province of Noord Brabant. After he had completed his business, the hospitable lady offered us a cup of tea and cake. Since her home was actually a small castle, I was anxious to see the inside so we accepted her offer gratefully. When I asked to use the washroom, I was astonished to see that the taps were actually gold. There was a bidet as well which I had never seen before and wondered what purpose it served. I asked my uncle later in the car and he explained it to me.

The weather had changed since we had left my grandparents' home and light snow was blowing in the wind. It was cold and damp. My uncle accused us jokingly that we must have brought this weather with us from Canada. The Netherlands seldom had snow during their winters and did not have snow removal equipment to deal with it.

As we returned to the car Uncle Gustaaf asked us if we would be interested in visiting the Canadian War Cemetery nearby. We were proud Canadian citizens by this time and so wanted to read the names of the soldiers who had given their lives to liberate Holland. As we came closer, we noticed a large American cemetery as well. Our car stopped at the gates of the Canadian Cemetery and all three of us debarked. My uncle told us of the Book of Remembrance in a small brick building at the far end. We signed our names along with comments about the park-like pristine beauty of the cemetery. Then we returned to the first row of graves. My mother walked to the right and I turned left and began to read the names, rank and ages of the men buried there. I was shocked to learn that most of them were my age of 23 or younger.

Suddenly, I noticed the name, "Clifford Thomas Donahue", Lance Corporal, of the Black Watch Regiment, who died on November 13, 1944, age 29, older than most. I stopped and read it again very carefully. I had been friends with a girl named Sharon Donahue in Lively and I remembered that she had told me that her Dad had been killed in The Netherlands during WWII. Could this be Sharon's father's place of rest? I called my mother to come and read this marker as well. We took some photos to show Sharon and her mother Ann when we returned to Canada.

When I arrived home in Creighton Mine, I called Sharon's mother, Ann Chornenky. She was now married to Walter Chornenky and still living in Lively. I told her of my discovery and she verified that indeed that was where her first husband was buried. Her daughter Sharon was now teaching out of town but Ann said that she would inform her of my discovery in Bergen op Zoom.

Recently, I met Sharon's stepfather and his second wife and related this story to them. He told me that Sharon had visited her father's grave at Bergen op Zoom and that he had been there as well. I asked Walter for Sharon's email address so that I could reconnect with her. To my astonishment he informed me that Sharon had died 5 years previously of cancer. I had not known that as our lives had diverged and we lost contact with each other.

In May 2010, Prime Minister Stephen Harper was participating in the 60th Anniversary Memorial Service at the Canadian War Cemetery in Bergen op Zoom. It was in that very graveyard that I had unexpectedly discovered a Lively man's grave, the father of my friend, who had given his life in the liberation of my homeland. That commemoration brought back memories of my visit there in 1965.

An Invisible Condition

IT WAS THE fall of 1969, I was 28 years old, mother of a five- year-old and one -year-old daughters and the sad feelings I was experiencing just would not lift. I had no idea what going on, as I had always been an optimistic person who enjoyed life. What was happening to me? It was frightening! Crying for no reason at all became the norm for me. Sleepless nights, lack of appetite, concentration so poor that I was unable to read, poor memory, finally unable to care for my precious little girls, were all signs we could not ignore. Alex did not know how to help me and I had no idea how to get over this myself.

Worrying about me caused Alex to phone his sister Lillian who was a public health nurse, for advice. He was extremely concerned and eventually afraid to go to work leaving me alone with our little ones. Lillian came immediately to spend some time at our home in Creighton Mine. Her son Marc who was about 8 months old accompanied her. Lillian suggested to Alex that he contact my mother in Wallaceburg to come to get Jacquie for the duration and Lillian would take Michelle to her home. She also suggested that Alex and I move in temporarily with their mother on Ontario Street so that I would not be alone in the daytime while he was at work. My mother—in—law agreed with this, as did my mother.

My husband took me to Emergency where we met with the psychiatrist on call, Dr. Eric MacLeod, on a Sunday afternoon. After talking with me for a long time, Dr. MacLeod finally gave us a name for what I was experiencing and used a term, which has stayed with me every day of my life since. Clinical depression was his diagnosis. It was and is horrible! Since there were no beds available in the psychi-atric ward, I remained at my mother—in—law's home and visited Dr. MacLeod at the hospital four times weekly, for a period of about six weeks. I lost a lot of weight. By trial and error, he discovered which medications were helpful to me so that eventually I was able to become a fully - functioning wife and mother again. The dreaded dark days were slowly lifting and I found new desires to return to my own home and resume my life as it had been before this episode. Dr. MacLeod insisted that I continue my medications as prescribed in order to stay well. Life slowly returned to normal for our family and we were grateful.

I experienced occasional periods of depression over the following years and with the assistance of our compassionate family physician, Dr. Peter Bayly, as well as Dr. MacLeod, I was eventually able to overcome them. However, in November of 1986, just six weeks after my beloved mother—in—law had passed away, my demons returned stronger than ever before. I had been unable to sleep the night of November 1st and had actually gone into the back yard to attempt to rake leaves even though they were already frozen to the ground. I returned inside and began to bake muffins for our church's bake sale. It was 3 am. While I was completing that task, my mind started to dwell on the death of Alex's mother. I remember clearly comparing her passing to throwing a stone into a lake causing rings to appear on the surface of the water. After a short while these rings disappeared as though nothing had happened. It struck me that it was as if Annette Guimond Fex had never existed as everyone had gone back to his or her work after a few days. Well, if I were no longer there it would be the same. People would miss me for a short time but then life would just go on as it had previously. So distorted was my thinking at that point that I did not even think of going upstairs to rouse Alex and tell him that I was "in trouble". Neither did thoughts of my three young daughters cross my mind. All I could think of was ending the pain I felt. I was so deep within that pain that I took a knife out of the drawer and attempted to cut my wrist making many shallow cuts. It was only when I saw the blood trickling down that I seemed to realize what was happening to me. I returned to bed then beside my sleeping husband who was totally unaware of what had transpired in the kitchen. At 7 am after having slept very little, I got up as the girls were beginning to stir. When Alex rose, I was wearing a long—sleeved housecoat hiding my wrist. While the children were eating their breakfast, my sleeve slipped and in horror he asked me what I had done. My memories of what happened after that are unclear but fortunately Dr. MacLeod was again on call at the General Hospital and I was admitted immediately as with the cutting I showed that I was a danger to myself. It did not matter to me at all at that point. Our daughters were all in school by then and Alex learned to do the laundry and all the other necessary tasks to keep the household going.

After the initial two weeks, I was allowed to go home on weekends. It was then that I began to realize the stigma attached to mental illness. Well—meaning friends and acquaintances said things like, "You look great!", implying, what was I doing in hospital. Even my siblings and parents could not understand why it was taking so long for me to be released. A broken arm or any physical illness would have been so much easier both for me and for my family. However, that was not my problem then.

Two of my teaching colleagues came to visit me one evening at the hospital and brought flowers, which I appreciated very much. However, the words spoken in surprise by one of them soon deflated me. Her comment was, "You know we just walked in here and no one stopped us nor asked us any questions!" She was very sincere in her feelings. I quickly replied that I was in a hospital not in jail! I learned a great deal about depression and about my relationships and myself during that three-month hospitalization. I also learned that no one should ever make any decisions at three o'clock in the morning! The definition of depression is, "anger turned inward". I learned that for me anger is most often the trigger emotion. It was a most important lesson.

When I returned home in February of 1987, it took some time for me to be able to resume my duties as wife and mother. The General Hospital had an excellent women's support program then. We met twice weekly with psychologists Vickie MacDonald and Jack Julian. With the advice of Dr. MacLeod, I attended that program for nearly two years. It is unfortunate that due to lack of funds, that program had to be discontinued after three years or so. There was such comfort there, as we all understood the importance of confidentiality, trust, but also the struggles experienced by a depressed woman in her everyday life.

I was able to return to teaching after this and felt well and whole again. An exciting feeling! Teaching always gave me back my self-confidence and self worth. There were some recurring depressive periods over the next years even some resulting in hospitalizations. Over the course of this time my psychiatrist concluded that for me depression was a chronic illness. It would keep recurring for the rest of my life. That was most upsetting for both Alex and me to hear. I was also told that I would need to take medications for the rest of my life. That was compared to a diabetic requiring insulin all of his or her life. Even though I came to know and understand that clinical depression is due to a chemical imbalance in the brain, it is still difficult to accept that the threat of it is life—long. Anxiety attacks are debilitating and I began to experience those as well. This condition is three times more common in women than in men. Symptoms include heart palpitations, sweating, dizziness, trembling, choking, feelings of unreality or being detached as if watching yourself from afar; numbness—all or any of these are frightening and caused me to isolate myself in my bedroom often. In this way I felt that I could avoid trigger situations. However, it is not possible to live this way for very long. Treatment for panic attacks is medication and cognitive therapy. More medication!

My most serious depressed time began early in 2001. Psychiatrist Dr. Zamar hospitalized me at the Algoma Hospital for about 7 weeks. Even after I returned home, I could not seem to become well again. That was upsetting. In May, I was hospitalized at Algoma Hospital again. I was seeing Dr. Zamar weekly during this time and even though he changed my meds several times, nothing seemed to help. In August, he suggested that I needed to go to Homewood Health Centre in Guelph for intensive therapy. There is always a long waiting period to be accepted at this world—renowned psychiatric hospital. By mid-October Dr. Zamar was totally out of patience with the admitting clerk and insisted that I be admitted as soon as possible. I heard this conversation myself as he made it from his office as soon as I entered for my appointment. On November 5, I was finally admitted. It was frightening, as I had no idea what to expect. The sessions were indeed intense and often very difficult as I was forced to face truths about my life, which I had avoided confronting previously. By doing so and receiving daily feedback, I learned new coping skills, which if I implemented them, should assist me in recognizing my problems before they became unmanageable. In all, I spent 11 weeks at Homewood—the most productive time in my life in helping me to live a happier and more constructive life. The day after I returned home, I wrote a list of the lessons I had learned there. I still refer to this list from time to time.

My struggle with mental health issues continues. I awaken some mornings in tears for no reason that I can discover. This is upsetting. Some mornings my mood is low and again I cannot always find the trigger that caused this. Sometimes this may last just one day or even part of a day but at other times my mood may not lift for several days. I try to apply the skills I have learned over these many years of treatment. Sometimes I'm successful. During these depressed times I feel totally dead inside—not happy, not sad, just no feeling at all. Fighting through these periods by keeping busy, writing, making myself attend things even though I have absolutely no interest in anything, occasionally will assist to dissipate the depression. Stress manifests itself as a heaviness which settles in my chest. Therefore, eliminating stressful situations is desirable. But this is not always in my control. It is imperative that I attempt to find the underlying cause of tension in order to try to lessen it. The feelings of hopelessness and helplessness, which I experience from time to time, always scare me, as I don't know how long they will last. The important fact is that I do understand now that they will pass, they are not permanent. That knowledge alone is a comfort to me.

SNOB HILL FUN

MY HUSBAND CAME home with exciting news from work one day in the mid-1960s. INCO had awarded us a company house on Wavell St.! Living in a house on locally nick-named "Snob Hill" in Creighton Mine in the sixties was everything a young family with a small child could hope for. The neighbours were extremely friendly and warm and made us feel at home immediately when we moved into a duplex in 1965. We just had one little daughter then, our Jacqueline whom we called Jacquie. Our next - door neighbours, Enci and Helen DiFilippo, lived in the other side of our duplex at 43B Wavell. Across the street lived Bill and Delores Mulligan and family, Ernie and Jackie Chenier as well as many other families: Ingrahams, Lynns, McAuliffes, Leblancs, Connors, Zadows, Trembleys, Larssons, Jamiesons, Lucks, Hurds, Murphys, etc. We soon became acquainted with everyone. In no time our neighbours were our friends as well.

Our new address was 43A Wavell St. We had two bedrooms and a bathroom upstairs, a spacious living room with a large picture window, a dining room and small kitchen on the main floor. The house also had a basement where the children could play and where we had our laundry facilities as well as our huge octopus oil furnace. Having moved here from a small two-bedroom apartment, we felt most fortunate to have so much more space! The lovely hardwood floors throughout the house added comfort and grace. We had a small front yard where I could indulge in my burgeoning passion for gardening. Tulip bulbs were the first flowers I planted along the front sidewalk. They were beautiful when they bloomed the following spring! In our backyard we were fortunate to have a small hill—perfect for children to roll down in the leaves with their squeals of delight! The gorgeous colours of the maple trees in the backyard in autumn were incredible! There was also a wonderful tall stone fireplace where we toasted marshmallows occasionally for whoever was around. It was also a safe place to burn the colourful leaves and enjoy that delightful scent in the fall and slide down with glee in the winter snow.

I became pregnant with our second daughter, Michelle, and the neighbours surprised me with a wonderful baby shower. My Mother had also assisted in many ways which was great! The remarkable gifts were much appreciated. My mother-in-law and sisters-in-law Madeleine and Marie Claire attended the shower as well. When Baby Michelle was born on June 11, 1968, our neighbours and friends came to visit the newest little Fex girl. Teenage girls Audrie Jamieson, Connie Larsson, Karen Mulligan, and Lillian Cozzarini became our trusted babysitters allowing us to go out without worry as the girls' parents were close by if a problem occurred with our precious little ones.

Our little girls, Jacquie and Michelle, were fascinated by the blue jays which dared to come close to the kitchen window where the children could watch them while eating their breakfast. It was excellent entertainment for all of us. In spring, seeing who spied the first robin was always an animated contest in our family. Alex's brother Norman built a playhouse for his little nieces who spent hours in there with Mom being invited for tea. The red swing set also provided much amusement for Jacquie and Michelle. Such innocent free pleasures! When our girls were a little older and playing with their friends on the street, we all looked out for all the children. If someone misbehaved, they would be scolded by whatever mom or dad happened to see the unacceptable actions. When a child fell, he/she was taken inside the nearest house to be washed, comforted and given a band aid and sent back out to play. If something more serious occurred, the parents were called or the child was brought home to be cared for. Our children were carefree and we parents had peace of mind knowing that someone was always around to keep an eye on the youngsters. Hallowe'en was a festive time on the "Hill" as we knew every child who came trick—or- treating to our doors. I had taught many of them at Creighton Mine Public School. They loved coming to their teacher's house as much as I enjoyed seeing them. Of course, they wanted me to guess their identity. Alex and I admired their creative home-made costumes and sometimes had them sing or dance for us. Such fun!

Everyone went down the farm road where my family used to live, to pick the ubiquitous, tasty blueberries in the summer for delicious pies or to sell for extra money for the family. For older children the near-by bush was a wondrous place to play all sorts of games during the long summer holidays. In winter, if someone became stuck in the snow on Wavell Street, immediately several men and older boys would come to assist the driver. Sliding down any hills to be found was a source of merriment all winter long. Skating on big and small ponds was great fun as well.

The adults enjoyed meeting occasionally for a cup of coffee or tea, sharing a meal together, and at Christmas time—perhaps a neighbourhood cocktail party to celebrate the season. Just meeting each other on the street and chatting was easy and comfortable as we all had so much in common. Our husbands all worked at the mine in varying capacities, which is why we lived in these company houses. We were all raising our children the best way we knew how.

We appreciated the deep sense of community which was Creighton Mine. Creightonites were most supportive of each other in good times and bad. Those were memorable years for our family and the many wonderful friendships we made have lasted to today.

Going Underground

WHAT IS IT like to go underground in a real mine? This was a question I had asked my Dad many times after he began to work deep down in Creighton Mine's #5 Shaft in 1952. "Oh, child, it is dark, hot and wet and very hard work", was his answer. Dad, who had been raised on a farm in Holland, disliked the mine from the very first day he went down. However, he had a wife and five children to support and since we had only been in Canada one year, he felt he had no choice. The money was good and the family desperately needed it. But the questions would not leave me alone.

My curiosity became even stronger when I began to teach at Creighton Mine Public School in 1962. The school was located immediately adjacent to Creighton's # 3 Shaft and we were keenly aware of the comings and goings there as we could observe everything from the playground. The fathers, uncles and grandfathers of my pupils worked in the mine. The curriculum in Grade 4 stated that I must teach what it was like in the mine so that the children would have a clearer understanding of conditions and jobs there. I found this difficult to do as I had never experienced visiting an actual operational mine. My husband worked in the office as a timekeeper and later a cost analyst. Occasionally he was given the opportunity to take the cage down so that he would have some idea of the working conditions underground. After he came home, I would ply him with questions that evening. His reply was always, "I'm just glad that I have an office job!"

In 1939, Queen Elizabeth and King George VI went down into Frood Mine. There was a superstition among many of the older miners that it was bad luck to have a woman go underground. Understandably the miners were upset. The area in Frood Mine which their Majesties visited was painted and carefully cleaned. INCO executives were on hand to welcome them and explain how hard rock mining was done here in the Sudbury Basin.

In the early 1970's Queen Elizabeth II and Prince Philip were also afforded the opportunity to visit this same Frood Mine which the Queen's parents had visited. In 1973, INCO management decided that the wives of the company staff personnel would be taken on conducted tours from time to time. In August, after the first group of women had been guided down into North Mine, I asked my husband to watch for an opportunity for me to experience going underground. Sometime later he called me from work. There had been a cancellation for the second tour at North Mine to take place on August 30—did I want to go? Of course, he knew what my answer would be! We were asked to be at the mine at 9 am. Then the mine safety supervisor asked us our names to ensure that we were indeed related to INCO employees. When he came to me, I replied that my name was Erna Fex, wife of Alex Fex. He took one look at my pregnant stomach and bellowed, "Fex, you didn't tell me your wife is pregnant!" Alex's reply, "You didn't ask." Alex accompanied Garnet Smith into the room where we getting robed in overalls, helmets, lights, safety belts, and gloves. My husband approached me and whispered that Mr. Smith was extremely nervous about my going underground because of my pregnancy. I had already gathered that!

Rene Dionne then took a group photo of the women and down we went in the cage. The area where we were taken was not a dangerous place. But we did get to see and feel the water dripping from the ceiling and that was not pleasant. For a minute or so all lights were turned off to give us an idea of total darkness conditions in the mine. This underlined why miners wear their helmets with lights at all times. The huge roof bolts supporting the face of the rock were pointed out and explained to us. Those same types of bolts are visible in the tunnel at Science North and underground at Dynamic Earth. We were shown the lunch room where we were given a small snack. It was explained that this is where the miners received their safety training.

During the whole experience many questions were posed and all clearly answered.

This pregnant lady had not fallen or caused any commotion to the mine supervisor's relief. He remained close to me the whole time we were on the tour. He was only too glad to hand me back to my husband. Alex wondered later if I had been the first pregnant lady to have gone underground. Can you imagine the reaction and consternation if I HAD tripped or fallen?

MOXAM DRIVE

IT WAS A wonderful place to raise our daughters! We had been contemplating buying a house for some time while living on Wavell St. in Creighton. On my way to school—Our Lady of Fatima in Naughton, I would pass this large red brick house facing the highway. It intrigued me because it had stood empty for a long time. I wondered why? Finally, one day I suggested to my husband that we should contact the owner Ken Mackinnon, to ask to see the house inside. An appointment was made and we visited 27 Moxam Drive. The house contained four large bedrooms and bathroom on the upper floor. On the main floor was the kitchen, a lovely formal dining room and a very spacious living room as well as a powder room and a small room which appealed to me immediately. We negotiated the price with Mr. MacKinnon, reached an agreement and found ourselves the proud owners of a house.

Excitedly, I phoned my parents to share the good news with them. They were very pleased and anxious to visit us in our new location. That would happen sooner rather than later for my mother. The week we were planning to move into the house, both of my daughters contracted chicken pox! In a panic, I called Mom to ask if she could come to our rescue. I was teaching full time, report cards were due, my kids were sick, I still had much packing to do—and thank goodness Mom said she was on her way! The next two weeks were a blur but somehow, we got moved in on November 28, 1972. Definitely we did not have enough furniture for this large house but that was not an immediate concern. I claimed the little room as my own—a room of my own—I was thrilled! I contacted my colleague John Raymond to come to build book shelves for me and panel the room. We put shutters on the windows, placed my desk and chair in the room and I luxuriated in my library and office. John also replaced the counter top and sinks in the kitchen and rebuilt some cupboards as well as renovating our powder room. Our first Christmas in our new home was a joyous one as my husband and I appreciated the fact that we had found a house we knew we would grow to love.

Our daughters, Jacquie (8) and Michelle (4) loved all the space! They soon made friends with the family next door which had five sons close in age to them. The youngest two were identical twins whom the girls could tell apart in no time but we still have difficulty doing so. The back yards on Moxam Drive are huge and the kids loved it! No one had erected fences. I revelled in planting flowers and shrubs in the spring. Alex had not realized just how long it would take him to cut all that grass as even our front yard was a substantial size.

We could not have asked for more congenial neighbours! Rhena and Paul Merrifield on our right, Ed and Cassie Fron on our left, Dewey and Essie Haley just around the corner, the Whelans, Albianis, Moxams, we soon discovered that what we all had in common was a strong sense of family and hard work. It was a great atmosphere in which to raise our children. Even though we lived close to the highway it was very safe as Moxam Drive was a crescent separating us from that busy road. There was also a deep ditch between our homes and the road. Our children were so busy playing with their friends that the highway was hardly noticed. At first Alex and I were aware of the traffic passing by but we soon grew accustomed to it.

The master bedroom faced the spacious backyard as did the girls' bedroom. The other large bedroom became a playroom and that turned out to be a great idea as the neighbourhood kids loved to come over on inclement days and holidays to play school or other games. I had been able to get a full-size blackboard which the school was discarding. The children all enjoyed being able to use that to draw or play games. I made sure that we always had a plentiful supply of chalk and real brushes just like at school. That playroom also served as the birthday party room for the girls. It was perfect and all the toys and mess remained in that one room. Two years later when our youngest daughter Allison was born, the other spare bedroom became a lovely bright nursery. This made it actually a home for me—bringing a new baby to the house on Moxam Drive.

Having such a large house meant that we could entertain to our hearts' content. It was the scene of many showers for our own daughters as well as the neighbourhood girls. Family gatherings at Christmas, birthdays, First Communions, and graduations—there was ample room for all kinds of celebrations. Our driveway accommodated six cars and all others parked along the road. Everyone driving by knew when the Fex family was having a party. When I turned 50, Alex and the girls had hired a huge electronic marquee which told the world driving by that I had reached that milestone and I was teased for days afterwards. When Alex turned 50 later, the front yard blossomed with 50 pink flamingos! They had been placed there during the night and so the sight met him as he left to go to work at 6:30 am. Our daughter Michelle had arranged for those.

We were fortunate to live in a neighbourhood where we all became such close friends. There inevitably were deaths and other misfortunes which befell our various families. When that happened, without discussion, someone would take it upon themselves to ensure that everyone was aware of the event. One person would go door-to-door collecting money for the affected family for flowers and their other various needs. The card on the flowers always simply stated, "Moxam Drive Neighbours". The neighbours gathered at the home of the unfortunate family to offer support, hugs, bring food, do dishes or help in anyway possible. As in life, there were times of joy and sadness and we were all there for each other. We were family in the truest sense of that word.

The 33 years we spent in that house were warm, interesting and eventful. Alex and I were happy to have raised our daughters in such a positive neighbourhood. Leaving the house in 2005 was difficult for me. It meant down-sizing drastically, moving into the city, saying goodbye to our home which had meant so much. However, it was time. Our girls had been gone for quite some time and the house was ready for a new family which needed the space. The family who purchased the house has four little boys and so another brood of children is making the house a home. That made me feel better.

House with Erna in front, election sign for my brother Frank de Burger1995.

Pink balloons to celebrate that our granddaughter Rachel had been born.

GRANDMOTHERHOOD

I LOVE BEING a Grandma! It has often been said that grandchildren are God's reward for being a parent. Becoming a grandmother has been a source of unending joy to me. Holding my first grandchild, Emily, in my arms, I felt absolute joy and a very deep love, an actual infusion of delight, appreciation, and infatuation with this tiny baby girl. She was immediately an important member of our family for always. I realized right away that my life had moved to a new but wonderful dimension.

Emily was born during the night in September in North Bay in 1988. She is the daughter of our second daughter Michelle and her husband Jamie. After holding her tearfully in our arms, Alex and I had to return to Lively to work later that morning. My principal asked me why there was a glow about me. Joyfully I reported to him that I had become a grandma. After school, I called my daughter and she enthused how good the baby was, that she just slept all the time and that she was finding it difficult to feed her. A warning bell sounded in my head. That brought home to me very clearly that once I had given birth, I would be a mother forever even into the next generations. As it turned out the baby had some problems and spent some time in the neo-natal intensive care unit. What a relief when I phoned my daughter a few days later and heard Emily lustily crying. The danger had passed and she was fine!

Michelle and Emily spent a great deal of time with us and so we watched this delightful baby girl grow. Each new development was a source of wonderment. Whenever Emily was at our home, I read to her every night. She'd crawl into bed with me while I was reading to her and the intimate feelings of having a child lie in my arms was a constant source of absolute delight. Emily reminded me of the sense of curiosity and discovery which children have.

When Emily was 7 years old, Rachel was born to our daughter Jacquie and her husband Scott in Toronto. This captivating little redhead immediately stole our hearts. Rachel with her infectious smile and laugh, presented us with the challenge of ensuring that we were part of her life. Thus, began the routine of Alex and I making frequent trips to see this baby girl. Whenever we were in Toronto, reading to her was a favourite activity. The wondrous smiles of recognition when we arrived at her home assured us that she knew us.

Our camp on the French River drew all of us together often during the summer months and gave Emily and Rachel the opportunity to play together. We enjoyed watching our two granddaughters chatting and trying to catch fish! Rachel developed into a talented Irish dancer and we attended many of her recitals and competitions. The huge smile on her face told us that she was really enjoying herself.

Then, Jacquie and Scott presented us with our first grandson. Jacquie called from the Delivery Room, "Mom, I had a baby boy!" We hurried to Toronto when Trent Alexander was 2 days old.

Grandpa Alex presented our first grandson with a small football, symbolic since Alex had played football with the Sudbury Spartans. Trent's parents were delighted! We soon observed that this little boy's interests were different from our little girls' interests. Catching frogs was a favourite camp activity. He loved mud! Keeping the knees in his pants was an on-going challenge for his Mom. Trent was most adept at construction with his Lego showing us that his visual perception is excellent. Trent taught us a great deal about little boys. Today that little boy is 6 feet 2 inches tall with a beautiful smile keen intellect and is very kind.

In September 2006, Matthieu, another grandson, was born to our youngest daughter Allison. He claimed his own special place in our hearts. He literally runs everywhere and engages whoever is around in his games. His love of his toy trains is evident. His long afternoon naps gave his mom a chance to rest. Now that he is older, he has become a talented hockey player. If he is playing while we happen to be in Toronto we drive to whatever arena where the game is being played to applaud him.

In October of 2008, Matthieu's baby brother Nicholas was born. We now have more little boys than girls. As Nicholas grew, he learned many things from his big brother—some good, some bad. We are so fortunate to have five healthy grandchildren! Nicholas is more mischievous and sometimes does things that we weren't aware were his interest. Hockey and other sports show the same athleticism as exhibited by his older brother. Naturally we go to see his hockey games too which often happen to be the same weekend as his brother's. It's lovely to see what good friends these boys have become.

Our great- grandson Aayden was born in November, 2009. Emily and Joe lived in our co-op complex for nearly 3 years so we enjoyed playing with him frequently. He knows us well. It's such fun to know and interact with the next generation of our family. When he sees me, he smiles and runs to give me a wonderful leg hug! Now that he is older, he has become quite talkative which we enjoy but at times makes his Mom, Emily, tired. Emily and Aayden come to visit us periodically and we enjoy that every time. Emily is a productive and caring adult and a devoted mother to her son. Recently, he was here and helped us harvest beans in our garden bed. Then Opa suggested he should dig out some potatoes too. He loved getting his hands deep in the dirt. Every potato was a discovery and he kept saying, "This is fun!" One of our friends dug some carrots out of his bed and gave them to Aayden. He couldn't wait to show his Mom all of his produce. Opa and Oma got such a kick out of his reactions! We always look forward to their visits.

Grandmotherhood is an experience which cannot be imagined but must be experienced to be understood.

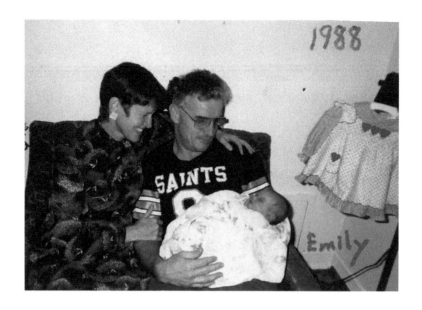

First grandchild, Emily

Matthieu, Rachel, Emily, Trent, Baby Nicholas – our grandkids , 2009

Being A Politician's Wife

LIFE TAKES UNEXPECTED turns at times. In the fall of 1974, several colleagues at work had been encouraging my husband to run for political office in the Town of Walden. Apparently, he had been mulling it over in his mind before he broached the subject to me. We have always supported each other in our ventures and this time would be no different. How would this affect our lives? Pros and cons considered, we decided that he would make the announcement.

That first campaign for the position of Councillor-at-Large in Walden was a learning experience for us. This position was the Deputy Mayor of Walden as well as a seat as a regional councillor in Sudbury. Alex went door—to—door to as many homes as possible beginning in September. Sometimes dogs attacked him and even tore his pants! He decided to act as his own campaign manager which made his life even busier. I soon found myself answering the phone, taxiing the girls to their activities, dragging baby Allison with me. The candidate was too busy. Meetings in our home with people who believed in Alex added to our activities. Then the first all candidates' meeting was announced. Alex and I discussed the importance of certain issues and wrote the speech. I'll never forget how nervous I was for that first meeting at Walden Arena! The place was packed and Alex acquitted himself very well.

I must admit though that there were times when I wondered what we had let ourselves in for. I was teaching full-time at Our Lady of Fatima School, which brought its own obligations with it. The children in the playground delightedly

.

---

would say, "Mrs. Fex, your daddy was at my house last night." They thought this was just great! Alex's slogan was "Mark your X for Alex Fex", and it caught on.

People would smile and say, "We know where to put our X". Alex's opposition was the incumbent Mrs. Gertrude Falzetta. Gertie was well—liked and a long-time resident of the Whitefish area. Her husband Frank was a businessman and also well regarded. To make a long story shorter, she beat Alex on Election Day by just 57 votes. Definitely, we were disappointed! However, such a small plurality of votes meant that we had to try again.

What lessons had we learned? Well, for one thing—Alex could not be his own campaign manager. It didn't make sense for him to be placing his own signs. His principal job was to hit the doors—as many as possible. Who should we ask? Since I had already been answering phone queries and doing a myriad of other tasks, it made sense that it be me. Our daughters, the two older ones, also got involved, as did their friends by folding two thousand leaflets for Alex to distribute as he went door-to-door. This made the whole enterprise fun for all of us. Their parents approved of these activities.

It was my job to organize meetings in all parts of the far-flung Town of Walden. We decided that "E—Day" would be at our home. Then we set to work preparing ads for the local newspaper. We sensed that support was growing. While campaigning in Lively, Alex met a group of four little boys carrying one of his signs which read, "Mark Your X for Alex Fex" and they were singing it as a song adding, "he's your guy!" He really got a charge out of that! The requests for signs in people's yards were more numerous than they had been before. Encouraging indications buoyed up our hopes.

Election day, December 6, 1976, finally dawned and oh no, we had a snowstorm!

Some roads in Whitefish were closed. It was a policy of Alex's to visit every polling station on Election Day. A friend drove him to Beaver Lake and on the return trip they noticed that a car was in the ditch. Alex and Matti Jousie helped the man get back on the road. As they were leaving, the man said to Alex, "I know where I'll put my X." Many people were unable to vote that day. Some of those were our supporters and some were Mrs. Falzetta's.

I had organized the day so that we had scrutineers at every polling station. Some were present all day, others for part of the day. They stroked off the names of voters after they had voted. They called our home where volunteers were also crossing off names. That's how we knew who of our declared supporters had voted and who might need a phone call to ask whether they needed a ride. This is referred to as "pulling the vote"—and it works! Some just needed a reminder that this was Election Day. Our scrutineers were present for the all- important vote count after the polls had closed at 8 pm. They were asked to call us with the results or bring them to our home.

As the phones began to ring at about 8:30 pm, volunteers recorded the results. Alex and I were too nervous to do this ourselves. Mrs. Ida Groulx brought us her winning results from Creighton. We knew that we had won that one! Next, our friend Lois Rauhala arrived from the 1-A Waters School but she wouldn't tell us anything until we gave her a beer. Yes, we had won that one too! Hopes were rising incrementally as we received these tallies. Even our daughters were getting excited. By 9:30 all numbers were in and Alex was the new Councillor-at-large and Deputy Mayor of Walden.

MCTV invited the winning candidates to come to the station. Our house was bursting at the seams with friends and supporters. They literally pushed us out the door. Reporter Joe Cook interviewed Alex and gave him the opportunity to thank our workers and supporters. I had indicated to Joe with a small sign that it was Alex's 35th birthday and he congratulated him on the air.

That first inauguration was wonderful and proved that our hard work had paid off.

Alex was re-elected 2 years later and two years after that he was acclaimed. In all, he served 6 years on Regional Council. In 1982, due to the untimely death of Regional Chairman Delki Dozzi, Walden Mayor Tom Davies was elected by the Regional Councillors to be the new Regional Chair. Subsequently, Walden Councillors elected Alex to be the mayor of Walden. That fall elections were held again. The times were different economically with interest rates at 20 to 22 %. The mood of the electorate was very negative. As a result, Alex and every mayoral incumbent in the province was defeated. Alex's opposition was Charles White who claimed that he would do the job for one half the salary. No other qualifications seemed important.

Alex put everything he had in running for election and he had worked extremely hard for his constituents after he was elected to represent them. The people in Dogpatch where my family had resided for 8 years, desperately needed municipal water. He was able to ensure that this happened for them. They were extremely grateful and thanked him very often.

As time went on, while our life became less harried, Alex felt he needed to try once more to become mayor. However, as the campaign progressed in 1985, and support showed up in unexpected sources, I was once again swept up in this venture. Without us knowing anything about it, Lively's David Scott had painted signs on the sides of his truck as well he had erected a huge billboard in his yard, "We need leadership! Nov. 12, VOTE ALEX FEX". Dave was at our home by 8 am every morning. "Well, Erna, what do you need me to do today?" Whether it was erecting signs, going to speak to someone, taking our daughters or me somewhere, Dave was available. One day during this campaign, Alex questioned something I had said. Dave replied very quickly, "Alex, Erna is your greatest asset!". Unfortunately, we lost this election. Dave was as devastated as we were.

Since then whenever an election is called, inevitably Alex is asked to run again. It was fun while it lasted and we made many friends whose efforts and support we appreciated. But we put that phase of our lives behind us forever.

Mayor of Walden – Alex Fex

Camp Life

It is my peace on earth!

In 1977, Civic Holiday weekend, Alex and I decided to take our three daughters for a drive. Where should we go? We hadn't driven towards French River for a long time and decided that would be our destination. The area had always been special to my husband and me as that is where we met in 1959. I was working at Pine Cove Lodge at the time which is located on Wolseley Bay. It is an absolutely beautiful area with very tall pines and cedars and rock outcroppings as well as the gorgeous waters of the French. We drove all the way to Pine Cove Lodge to show our daughters exactly where it was that their parents met so long ago.

On our way back along Turenne Road, we noticed a sign saying, "Cottage for Sale". We had been thinking of purchasing a camp for some time so decided to turn in to have a look at this cottage. The vendor, Mr. Emile Guy, was just showing the camp and the property to another family so we walked down to the water's edge. As we started to go back up, I instantly fell in love with this place. The enormous pines and cedars captured me and I remember saying to Alex, "Whatever the camp looks like inside is not important—we could never plant these trees in our lifetime!" He agreed with me and the decision was made then and there that we would make an offer on this property.

When Mr. Guy had finished with the previous couple, we were able to enter the actual building. It was perfect for our family as it had two bedrooms, a spacious living-dining—kitchen area, a porch with a bathroom and shower and was fully furnished. Since we have three girls, one bedroom for them was sufficient. The two younger girls would sleep in the bunk beds and our eldest daughter would occupy the single bed. There was a double bed in the other bedroom for us. The floor to ceiling picture window in the living room afforded us an excellent view of the waters of Ranger Bay. We informed the owner that we were extremely interested in purchasing this cottage that very day. Within three days, the deal was completed and the camp was ours.

We packed the car and hurried to our new summer home the first free weekend available. Our girls were 11, 8 and 3. Before we arrived, our vendor/neighbour to the right, had placed a small bouquet of wild flowers on the table as well as a WELCOME sign. What a wonderful way to greet us!

Just before we left to go home on Sunday evening, there was a knock at the front door. Curious as to who it might be, we received the best possible surprise! It was the neighbouring family who had come to introduce themselves—the Fitzgeralds. The best part about that was that their children matched ours in ages perfectly! Leslie was Jacquie's age, Frannie was Michelle's age and Gina was just a little older than our Allison. Their son Paul fit in between Jacquie and Michelle. Rose and Bill were close to Alex and me in age. We could not have asked for more congenial and like—minded neighbours! With our children matching so well in age, we realized that importing friends from home would not be necessary. That was a wonderful unexpected bonus!

They lived at their camp for the entire summer and we moved to ours as well. During the week our husbands travelled to work in Sudbury from our cottages. Rose and I were nearly the same age and so immediately we had much in common besides our kids. Our three girls and their three girls and one boy became good friends and are still friends today as adults. During the week Rose and I took turns observing the children as they played and swam. Actually, we needed to watch them together because there were seven kids of varying ages and that's too many for one mom to track. A number of times the mothers and children climbed the very high Ranger Bay hydro hill to pick blueberries. While the berries were delicious, we decided to stop doing that as that hill seemed higher and higher. As the years went by it became too exhausting especially for Rose and me.

On Saturdays, both families attended Mass in Alban, came home for supper and then we all gathered at our camp or at theirs, for cards or board games. Meanwhile, the adults enjoyed a glass of wine or a drink and interesting conversation. Bill's parents also spent many summers there with their camper parked close by. Quickly they became our friends as well. Poppa loved to tell ghost stories to the kids and they were enthralled to the point that ours were afraid to return home sometimes, crossing the empty lot between the two camps after dark. There was an abandoned decrepit shack on that property and Poppa's stories often involved that old (haunted) place.

The children loved to try to catch the alluring fireflies and put them in a jar with a lid to examine them more closely. Frogs were everywhere but it was their tadpoles which were so interesting. Every year a Mama Duck came swimming by the dock with her numerous ducklings. The kids fed them pieces of bread and delighted in watching the little ones compete for the food. We found out later that feeding the ducks bread was not a good idea!

We frequently observed the beautiful, graceful great blue heron leave the nest and launch himself into the sky. It was fascinating to watch as he circled going higher and higher until we could no longer see him. Many other birds made their presence known in early morning or at night. Such a pleasure to hear the varying songs! Fishing became a favourite activity for some and the excitement when a fish was caught was enjoyed by everyone. Campfires were always inviting, and many marshmallows were toasted and consumed. The kids from ages three to thirteen happily gathered wood for those campfires. The numerous annoying mosquitoes didn't prevent anyone from having fun.

We could hardly wait to start the camping season the following Spring. As early as we could, we drove from Lively to see how the camp had weathered the winter. Opening up our place that first Mothers' Day weekend was so delightful! From then on, we were at camp every weekend until the end of June. We moved there completely the Canada Day weekend and lived at camp until Labour Day.

Reluctantly we went home for the day once a week to do laundry and buy needed groceries. Watching our daughters enjoying swimming, campfires, board games on rainy days, becoming ever closer friends with the Fitzgerald kids next door, made Alex and I realize that we had made the correct decision in purchasing this cottage.

The children had abundant wonderful experiences at camp which created incredible memories for us all. They were exposed to things they would never have experienced at home. Our camp became a precious second home and Alex and I are most gratified that we made the decision to become camp-owners in 1977. Hard to believe that was forty years ago. Those were halcyon summers for the two families.

Our friendships have become life-long alliances which are happily renewed every summer. Now that most of the children have married, their spouses have also all become friends and we are enjoying meeting the next generation coming to the French.

The arrival of our own grandchildren has been a source of unending joy to us and their parents have happily introduced them to the French River experience from the time they were tiny babies. Our captivating first grandchild, Emily, expanded our enjoyment of camp in a whole new direction. Fascinating Rachel brought her own sense of delight to the camp experience, especially pretending to be a mermaid. Our first grandson Trent has been the adventurer finding totally different things to do than his female cousins. Watching the children discovering frogs and mud and of course learning to swim and dive has been such fun for us. Our son-in-law Scott loves to fish and his daughter Rachel can often be found in the evenings bonding with her dad on the dock while both are enjoying this peaceful activity. The entire family enjoys competitive games of Dutch shuffleboard which entails firing small wooden discs down towards small entry holes to cheers and jeers from everyone in the room.

We purchased a small motorboat and this allowed us to explore the river and revel in the beauty of our surroundings in all seasons. My husband and I loved to go for a ride in the early evening when there is not much traffic on the water and we can take our time enjoying the experience of the still environment. The haunting calls of the loons and the whippoorwills add to the general ambience of the evening.

Alex and I often comment that as soon as we drive up our steep driveway, our cares fall away and immediately we both experience peaceful mindsets. We sleep well at camp and so awaken refreshed to greet the day whether it is sunny or not. It really doesn't matter. For me it is the absolute best place to read and my husband enjoys doing puzzles. In the forty-some years since we have owned our camp, we have never allowed a television to intrude into our slow-paced world there. When we are there by ourselves, we appreciate the quiet atmosphere and thoroughly enjoy each other's company. The radio is usually on in the background and we do have a telephone to keep in touch with the outside world if necessary. It really is our haven.

1977

2007

Camp 1977– 2007

STRANDED ON THE FRENCH

THANKSGIVING WEEKEND WE usually close up our camp for the winter. While I know it is necessary to do this, I always find it bitter-sweet.

One Saturday, we drove down Highway 69 to the turnoff to Highway 64 to Alban, then onto Turenne Road to our camp driveway. The beautiful fall colours of the leaves made for a pleasurable drive on this rainy day. Exploring the amazing French River, the route of Samuel de Champlain in the 1600's, has always been a source of interest to us. Alex wanted to take a last long boat ride to the Ouellette Rapids to show our friends where he and most of our family members (not me!) had body—surfed the rapids wearing life jackets.

It was uncharacteristically quiet on the river this Thanksgiving weekend. Very few people were at their camps or boating on the river. The motor performed admirably and we reached the rapids in about 30 minutes. It was a smooth ride as the water was very still, just the way we love it! The colourful trees were reflected in the water and it was absolutely magical! All debarked to have a closer look at the rapids. Then it was time to return to camp to take the boat out of the water. That's when we got a most unwelcome surprise! When Alex started the motor, it growled just as in a car when the battery is low and that is what indeed it was! We were totally unprepared for that.

There was nothing to do but start paddling. The men paddled as fast as they could which was not very fast at all. The rain kept pouring down and in no time, we were all soaked. However, our spirits were not dampened and we told many jokes and we regarding the whole debacle as an adventure. Much laughter and teasing helped lighten the situation immeasurably. "Let's pull into shore right there! That looks like a good spot!" The men directed the disabled boat to the land. The rocks were slimy! More laughter! More dampness too! Alex tried to start the motor again. No luck! Not only did the motor not start but now we were hung up on the rocks so paddling was impossible. Our friend climbed out onto the bow of the boat, I moved as far forward as possible and the men managed to push us out from the offending rocks. Once more we were on our way. More reasons to laugh about our worsening situation.

Slowly we proceeded down the river. Finally, as we came around a bend, we spotted a cottage where a lady was tending a fire and her husband was on the dock. Hurray! We called out to him for help. Apparently, he had noticed our predicament already and was waiting for us to come closer. He had no boat to come to our assistance. He insisted that we go up to his cottage right away to get warm while he attempted to help the guys start our motor with his small generator. Gratefully, we followed his advice and greeted his wife who invited us in. We considered ourselves most fortunate that this couple was at their cottage. We introduced ourselves and learned that the lady's name was Lynn. She made hot chocolate for us to help us warm up. We appreciated her efforts and accepted thankfully. A short time later the three men came up to the cabin as they had been unsuccessful in starting the boat. That battery was dead! Paul introduced himself to us and told us that they lived in Barrie. After pouring a drink for himself and our men, he told us that he was a builder and was constructing this amazing three—storey cabin himself. They expressed their love for the French River which immediately gave us a shared inter-est. Conversation flowed easily. Paul and Lynn Comuso were indeed gracious hosts as well as being our rescuers.

When we had warmed up, Paul drove us to our camp in his truck. The women stayed there while Alex picked up our extra battery and both guys returned with Paul to try to rescue our boat. After a while, we heard the familiar sound of the motor bringing the guys back to our dock. Our adventure had ended safely and what could have been a drastic situation had turned into a story we would tell our families eagerly.

By now it was getting dark, and getting the boat out of the water would have to wait for another day.

A Patient Advocate

MY MOTHER, ALICE de Burger, required complex health care in her seventies and had to be admitted to a nursing home. She had been diagnosed with a terminal illness several years before and the disease had progressed to the point where we had to make this difficult decision. When I realized the necessity, I became my mother's advocate willingly.

The Fisher-Lapointe Nursing Home was just down the street from my parents' home on Nelson Street in Wallaceburg. This made it convenient for Dad and us to visit her. We knew living there was a difficult adaptation for her. Before her illness, as she and I walked by she would express that she never wanted to be there as a patient. With time, Mom became resigned to the fact that this was her home "for now". I would agree that this was so. At other times she would cry, "I have no home anymore!" This was very difficult to hear. It made me want to cry as well. However, my answer always was, "That is not true, Mom, your home is still just down the street at 622 Nelson St."

Whenever she wished, we would take her home for a few hours in the afternoon. She enjoyed napping in her own bed surrounded by the people and things she loved. I would ask her what she would like me to make for dinner and cook the meal in the Dutch way as she had always done. However, sometimes she would awaken from her nap and state that she wanted to return to the nursing home immediately. That puzzled us at first, but we soon realized that she was either very tired or was exerting a little power in the only way as yet open to her, at home.

My mother had always been a strong independent woman and she knew that she was becoming weaker steadily. She was frightened. We could see it happening and tried our best to help her in any possible way. We visited Mom as frequently as possible always at different times of the day—often several times a day. We felt that by going at unexpected times, Mom's care would have to measure up all day. That turned out to be an excellent idea. I went for a walk to pick up the London Free Press early in the morning and always stopped in to say "Good morning" and ask if she had spent a good night. She loved seeing me first thing in the morning with a hug and a kiss. Dad went to visit every afternoon and he would bring her some fresh fruit which she loved. In their Dutch upbringing, fresh fruit was a staple.

One day when Dad and I were ready to go to the nursing home, I noticed him again filling up a bag with fruit for Mom. I asked my Dad how much it was costing for Mom to be in the nursing home. She was in a semi-private room as she had requested, as she loved company. I was aghast when Dad said the cost was $1,500 per month—this was in 1996. Then why did we feel the need to augment her diet?

When we arrived, I asked the nurse why my mother was not getting much fruit. She sent me to the dietitian who assured me that the patients were indeed given fruit after meals and for snacks. I asked her to tell me what she meant by "fruit" and she stated that the patients were given canned pineapple, apple sauce, fruit cocktail, etc. She also told me that the food allowance for each patient was $ 4. a day. I asked her to repeat that to my Dad who became upset. It was especially disturbing as the Wallaceburg area is surrounded by fruit orchards of all kinds! I then asked her what it would take for my mother to receive real fresh fruit. Her answer made me realize that I should have checked into this situation sooner, "All the patient or her family has to do is ask!" My reply obviously was, "We are asking". The next day Mom was given her snack while I was there visiting. That banana was so long that DEBURGER was printed on it in black magic marker! We both laughed. After that she was given grapes, apples, oranges and peaches in season. That was certainly an indication to us that we needed to be looking out for her all the time.

The next episode occurred just weeks before Mom's death. I arrived before noon on a Tuesday and saw immediately that she was upset. When I asked her why, she raised her long sleeve and to my astonishment, her arms were all black and blue. I was shocked! In her weak voice, she said that she did not want any more needles as they were too painful. Just then a lab technician came into the room to take blood. I asked her why. The doctor had ordered it and so she had to do it. I explained that my mother had clearly stated that she did not want any additional needles and asked her to leave Mom's room. At that point, I heard the nursing home's Dr. Thorner's voice in the hallway. (I knew he always visited on Tuesdays.) I met him in the corridor and informed him of my mother's wishes. His reply," Well, let's go and see what Alice says." After she verified what I had told him, he cancelled the order.

Mom had signed a DNR order so the staff knew that she just wished to live out her final days without pain. She died peacefully in her sleep on March 3, 1997 at age 76.

The lesson we all learned is that when a loved one is institutionalized someone in the family must become that patient's advocate. It's imperative!

WORLD JUNIORS—1988

IT WAS AN experience that we will never forget! We heard the call for volunteers for the World Juniors on radio and Alex decided that he would look into it to see what the volunteering entailed. When he returned home, he was very excited and said to 14- year-old Allison and me, "Let's all get involved, I think we'll really enjoy it!" He told me they needed people who could speak different languages. He had asked if a team was coming from The Netherlands and was told yes. The next day we returned to the planning office on Lisgar Street and offered our services pointing out that Alex and Allison spoke French and that I spoke fluent Dutch.

The World Junior Championships in Athletics II were to occur from July 22—July 31, 1988, at Laurentian University. All of the athletes were 16 and 17 years old. The first contest had taken place in Greece the previous year. Young athletes from 120 countries were expected to participate in Sudbury in 1988. The immense task of organizing a complex competition of this magnitude was begun more than a year ahead of time. More than 1000 athletes and support staff members were expected.

The Volunteer Command Centre was located at Huntington College. We each received an accreditation badge, which we had to wear at all times while we were on duty at the Championships. We needed it to access our designated areas as well as any volunteer services. We were issued specific uniforms consisting of navy- blue pants and a light blue polo shirt, which had the official logo, imprinted on it, as well as our own white running shoes. We were also advised that we would have to pay to attend any events in which we were not directly involved.

Many fundraising events were held previous to the actual event. The biggest one was a Beach Boys Concert, which also featured Roy Orbison, a favourite of ours. There was a huge crowd and the three of us enjoyed ourselves immensely! At one point I glanced at our daughter and she was dancing to the same tunes as we were. Such fun!

Lionel Courtemanche was in charge of the wonderful Opening and Closing Ceremonies and attendance at the practices was mandatory for all those involved. That included the three of us as we had been assigned to be hosts for various teams. Alex was host for the Russian Team, (we never did find out why), Allison had the Lebanese team (who spoke French) and I was hostess for the Dutch team as I had requested.

Alex was working graveyard shift on July 24, the day our teams arrived at the Sudbury Airport. I had gone to the airport by shuttle bus when the Dutch team arrived. I was tremendously excited and had even prepared a welcome sign for them in Dutch on Bristol board. After my credentials had been checked I was allowed to board the plane to introduce myself to the team I would be hosting. They were very surprised and pleased when they heard me address them in Dutch! They had not expected that at all! The team consisted of 15 athletes and 7 leaders including: head of the Royal Dutch Athletic Association (KNAU), a doctor, physiotherapist, three male coaches, and one female coach. We all deplaned and boarded the bus, which took us to Lockerby Composite School for registration and accreditation. That process was far too lengthy and by the time it was completed it was 3 am! Considering that the team had arrived at the airport at 9 pm, and had been en route all day they were extremely tired and somewhat cranky. They wanted nothing more than to find their beds at the university residence which had been christened the "Athlete's Village" for the duration.

The next morning, we were at that Athlete's Village by 9 am. I was met with questions and problems as soon as I arrived. The physiotherapist's massage table had not arrived with the rest of the luggage; their coffee machine adapter did not work and the adults needed their coffee; Esther, the female coach required a single bed; what are the pool hours; when and where could they play tennis; etc. A few phone calls solved most problems but not that of the coffee machine. When I ran into Alex and told him that he drove home to Lively to get our own coffee maker for them. They were most appreciative! After that he was as welcome in the Dutch quarters as well as I was!

I was invited to attend the first technical meeting of the team. To my surprise and great pleasure, they made me an honorary team member. This meant that I could attend all of their strategic meetings during the competition. As their hostess it was up to me to apprise them of all the amenities available at the university. Things such as the convenience store, post office, phone centre, bank, laundry facilities, hair dresser, medical centre, games room, linen exchange, command centre and of course the dining hall and its hours, were all of varying importance to the youth and their leaders.

Alex's problems as host of the Russian Team were very different. The biggest problem he faced was the language barrier. This made it extremely difficult for him to communicate with the 90-member team members. He soon discovered that the Russian athletes' passports had been confiscated before they got off the bus at the Athlete's Village. He was certain that this was done to prevent defection during or after the games. The coaches pretended not to understand English but they navigated the site very well. When the athletes and staff realized that Alex had his car at the university, they convinced him to take some of them to a Future Shop where they purchased "ghetto-blasters". Jeans was the other item of great interest for the Russian youth. He chauffeured several of the coaches and the lone interpreter to South Ridge Mall where they bought some inexpensive items at a yard sale.

Finally, it was time for the Opening Ceremonies. On July 26, we gathered at the Athlete's Village at 5 pm and walked with our assigned teams to the soccer field with the ceremonies to begin at 7 pm. I carried the sign for Holland; Alex did so for Russia and Allison for Lebanon. The flag bearers for each team were the team captains. The mood was exciting and festive.

Numerous people as well as many media members were taking photos. I asked Esther Goedhart to take a picture of me with the Dutch flag. It was a sentimental yet meaningful gesture on my part appreciated by the Dutch coaches. The teams entered the packed stadium in alphabetical order and were welcomed by loud applause. I was so very proud to walk at the head of the team from The Netherlands. The USSR Team led by my husband received a warm welcome. As is the custom, the team representing the host country, Canada, entered last to thunderous applause, cheering, and flag waving. It was an intoxicating feeling to participate in all of this!

A hilarious incident occurred when Alex needed to bring something to the Dutch Team's quarters in the Athletes' Village. He knocked on the door and was told to enter. As he described it to me later, he couldn't believe his eyes—physiotherapist Hans Heymeskamp was giving a massage to Yvonne van der Kolk who of course was nude from the waist up. Neither the athlete nor the physio were the least bit disturbed by Alex's presence and continued their activity but Alex didn't know where to look he told me afterwards.

The team leaders from The Netherlands were most upset to learn that even though I was their accredited hostess I was not allowed to watch the competitions unless I paid the expensive entry fees. Rien Stout, the Chef de Mission was in fact outraged and he and Joop van Drunen who was the head of the Royal Dutch Athletic Union, (Koninklijke Nederlandse Atletiek Unie - KNAU), accompanied me to see accreditation officer Gary Polano, and informed him that they needed me in the stadium with them in case translation was required if something came up. The necessary accreditation was granted. I was elated to know that now I was able to really be an active part of the delegation wherever they wanted me to be with them. Alex did not receive this accreditation and so ended up spending more time with our Dutch friends than with his assigned team.

The competitions were exciting as these young athletes were the best in the world in their age groups. Whenever both a Canadian athlete and a Dutch athlete were competing in the same event, I must admit that my loyalties were divided. The Dutch members would look to see for whom I was cheering. July 1988, was the hottest July on record at the time and sitting in the stands demanded wearing a hat and plenty of sunscreen. I continued to wear my official shirt but changed into shorts due to the excessive heat, rather than the hot polyester pants which had been issued. Some of the events were changed to evening due to the heat. It was too dangerous for the competitors some of whom had already passed out or had suffered heat stroke keeping the paramedics busy.

Science North offered the athletes free admission on July 27 provided of course that they were not competing or training that day. There were barbecues, swimming parties at Lake Laurentian, disco parties, and many other events for the participants every evening. Allison really enjoyed mingling with the athletes who were not much older than she was. Alex and I visited with the Dutch leadership after the races had been completed for the day getting to know them and hearing about their experiences while they wondered about the Canadian way of life. One morning I showed them some blueberry bushes on the grounds. They loved the taste of the wild berries! I had some at home and that evening when I went home, I baked several dozens of blueberry muffins to have with coffee the next day. They absolutely loved them and were most appreciative of my efforts especially in that heat!

I discovered that Esther's birthday was on July 30. I suggested to the other adults that we surprise her with a party. They agreed enthusiastically so I ordered a large birthday cake from Cecutti's for her. When I told the bakery who the cake was for, they gave me a huge discount. I presented Esther with a picture book showing Canadian scenes, which she said she would treasure. It was a fun evening and we had managed to surprise her even though all of the athletes knew of the plan.

Esther and I had connected almost as soon as we met especially so when we realized we were from the same province in Holland (Zeeland), were born the same year and had even been married the same year! We were immediately comfortable with each other. We promised to stay in touch after the games and we actually have!

When the Closing Ceremonies were over on July 31, it was time to say goodbye to my new friends. They presented me with beautiful gifts of appreciation. I received an exquisite pair of wooden shoes specially carved for the KNAU and a lovely oval Delft blue vase. Because Alex had been so helpful to the Dutch team, the organizers gave him a very expensive bottle of the best Dutch gin, called Bittenberg, in a wooden case. He had also received a book in Russian from his Russian team and some pins.

Christmas of 1988, we received Christmas cards from every member of the team from The Netherlands again expressing their appreciation for what we had done for them. Esther and I had corresponded several times by mail and she made me promise to visit her the next time I travelled to my homeland. Each time since then that I have gone to Holland we have always spent time together.

Alex, Allison and I had spent at least 12 hours a day at the venue and enjoyed ourselves thoroughly! Now that it was all over, we had no regrets but we were totally exhausted and all three of us literally collapsed on the bed! It was truly an unforgettable experience!

Erna with the Dutch flag

MOMENTOUS NEWS

MY ELDEST GRANDDAUGHTER, Emily, called to ask if I would like to accompany her to the New Sudbury Shopping Centre one day. I agreed immediately. We have always had our special "Grandma and Emily Days" and I was so very pleased that she wanted to do that once again. As usual we talked and enjoyed each other's company as we always have. Little did I know how special the day would be. I had asked her for gift ideas for her upcoming graduation from Cambrian College as we wandered in and out of several stores. She didn't show much interest in shopping.

After about an hour we returned home. When we were quite close to my home, Emily looked straight ahead and announced that she had news for me. "I am pregnant, Grandma", she said in a trembling voice. Immediately, I felt tears in my eyes and realized that what I was about to say was tremendously important to our relationship from that minute on. She shyly looked at me to ascertain my facial expressions. I was acutely aware of all of this in the split second while I was considering how to react to this momentous news. "Honey, a new baby in the family is wonderful and exciting news", was my reply. She heaved a huge sigh of relief! "I have been so worried about telling you!!" she blurted. Next question, "How do you think Grandpa will feel?" I assured her that he would be every bit as positive as I had been. When we arrived at home, she told him the same way she had revealed the news to me. Immediately, he gave her a huge hug and again I saw the tension leave her. We told her that we would not only love her baby but welcome it into our family with open hearts. Emily then began to talk about her pregnancy. She said that she had just completed the first trimester and that the baby was due early in December. She had not experienced any morning sickness and continued to talk constantly how she and Joe, the baby's father, had been planning for this baby.

Emily and Joe had moved into an apartment together on Kelly Lake Road and they were very excited to show it to us. She was very happy with Joe, and we liked him though we were just getting to know him. We noticed how caring he was, respectful, pleasant and easy to relate to. Emily's mom, Michelle, liked him too and since Em and her mom are very close, that was most important to her.

The realization that I would soon become a great—grandmother sank in after she had left. "Me? A great - grandmother?" Alex suggested that we go in and toast our new status as great—grandparents. I readily agreed and with tears in our eyes, we enjoyed a celebratory drink of Grand Marnier. Another wonderful phase of our lives had begun. Our granddaughter would soon have a child of her own! It is difficult to comprehend this wonderful, incredible news fully as yet.

On July 21, she excitedly came to show us her ultrasound pictures and we learned that we were awaiting a great grandson. From then on, I began to pick up blue baby items. I had already begun to crochet a white baby blanket as I had for all my grandchildren. Emily continued to include us in pregnancy developments and I appreciated that. One day she came over to ask if I wanted to accompany her and Joe to the obstetrician to listen to the baby's heartbeat. Overwhelming emotions and a few tears were my reactions.

Emily and Joe moved into Carlin Co-op where we lived, on November 28. That very night her water broke and her baby was on the way. Good thing that I had completed crocheting that blanket! At 11 am the next morning Alex and I rushed to the hospital to see how our granddaughter's labour was progressing. Her Mom, Michelle, promised to call us as soon as the baby was born. Anxiously we waited all day and finally at 11:30 pm she called with the exciting news. Baby Aayden Alexander Robidoux was born on November 29, 2009 and he and his Mommy Emily, were well. He weighed just 5 lb.5oz. We couldn't wait to meet him the next morning.

As I stood there holding this tiny baby boy in my arms, I looked over at my granddaughter who was cradling her baby in her arms and just glowing. It became real. I was now a great grandmother and was totally in love with our new baby.

Emily and Baby Aayden

CHARLES AND DIANA
VISIT SUDBURY

IT WAS 1991, October 24, to be exact, and there was great excitement in the City of Sudbury. Prince Charles and his beautiful wife, Diana, Her Royal Highness the Princess of Wales, were being officially welcomed to Ontario, in our city. Premier Bob Rae's decision to do so was welcomed with enthusiasm by our mayor Peter Wong, City Council and all Sudburians.

To my exquisite delight, my husband and I had received an official invitation to be inside Science North to see them up close. I was so excited that I had hardly slept the night before! Previously, I had done some serious shopping because after all, meeting royalty required a new dress of course. It took me a while but finally at Elm Fashions, I found two dresses which I thought would be suitable. Feeling rather guilty, I decided to purchase a new tie for my husband for the event. It was the least I could do!

We were placed (and I do mean placed), on the top floor of Science North close to the elevator. With us were Maurice Switzer, publisher of the Sudbury Star; a member of the Crown Attorney's office, and three others. Of course, we had undergone a thorough screening beforehand and were instructed clearly that we were not allowed to have cameras inside the building. The other reminder we were given was that it was not proper to address the Royal Couple unless they spoke to us first.

Finally, Prince Charles, Premier Bob Rae, Mayor Peter Wong, and several other men whom I did not recognize, emerged from the elevator. They passed by us very quickly, nodding in our direction. Then the moment I had been waiting for arrived! There she was, Diana, even more beautiful in person than in the media, stepping out of the next elevator. She was accompanied by Arlene Perly Rae, wife of the premier, Mrs. Wong, and I presume several ladies-in-waiting. Princess Diana stopped directly in front of me, smiled, and we made direct eye contact. I smiled back brightly at her. It seemed ridiculous not to be able to speak to her! After she and her entourage had moved on, my husband who had amusingly watched my brief encounter with my idol, asked me if I wished I had spoken to Diana. "Yes!" was my instant reply. He took my hand and pulled me to a spot down further in the building near the theatre, and we waited for her Royal Highness to pass by again. Shortly thereafter her group approached and once again she stopped exactly in front of me.

Throwing caution to the wind (after all what could "they" do to me), I said to her, "Thank you for coming to Sudbury." She dazzled me with her smile and her gorgeous blue eyes, stuck out her ungloved hand in a firm handshake, and replied graciously, "Thank you for inviting me!" You can imagine my excitement!

My husband and I returned to our assigned spots where we related what had happened to the others. Maurice Switzer, noticing the glow on my face and the sparkle in my eyes, regretted that no camera had been present to capture that special moment. So was I. The memories have not faded for me, neither have the wonderful emotions I experienced that day. It is truly one of the highlights of my life which I will never forget.

It was a horrible shock to me when she was killed in Paris just six years later in 1997 in a tragic car accident in Paris. Watching her young sons walk behind her casket a week later was terribly sad and very emotional. The fact that the grounds in front of her home at Kensington Palace were buried under thousands of flower bouquets proved that she was indeed the "People's Princess." The fact that her Royal Highness title had been taken from her when she divorced Prince Charles meant nothing to her place in people's hearts.

In honour of
Their Royal Highnesses
The Prince and Princess of Wales

Ontario

The Honourable Bob Rae
Premier of Ontario
and Arlene Perly Rae

request the pleasure of the company of

Mr. and Mrs. Alex Fex

at a Reception
on Thursday, October 24th, 1991 at 11:30 a.m.

Science North
100 Ramsey Lake Road
Sudbury, Ontario

Dress: Business Attire

R.S.V.P. by October 18th
Office of Protocol (416) 325-8509
Long distance calls accepted

PLEASE PRESENT THIS CARD FOR ADMITTANCE TO SCIENCE NORTH

THE GRADUATE

It was a life—long dream of mine and finally in June of 2000, it was a fact. I, Erna de Burger Fex, at the age of 59, was a university graduate with a BA in Sociology.

It had been a very long journey. Life intervened constantly with children's problems, and my own illnesses interrupting my studies but I had persevered and I was proud of that fact. I began my studies in the summer of 1962 after graduating from North Bay Teachers' College.

Laurentian University was spread out all over downtown Sudbury in those days. I remember that my first course, French, was in a room on Durham St. above a business. The spirit of adventure existed in all of us in those early days of Laurentian University. The actual buildings of the university were rising on the Sudbury horizon between two scenic lakes—Lake Laurentian and Ramsey Lake. It was, and is, and gorgeous setting for this institution of higher learning. The architects, engineers and planners kept the surroundings in mind as they designed the buildings of stone with many windows letting the outside in. The forests of evergreens, oaks, birches and maples in the area formed a lovely backdrop for the edifices. All Sudburians were justifiably proud of our university when it officially opened its doors in 1964.

My university studies were sporadic after that first course. Marriage, raising children, working full—time, there did not seem to be enough hours in the day to be taking courses as well. However, my dream never waned. Someday I would finish

I promised myself and become a university graduate. In the meantime, my three daughters, Jacquie, Michelle and Allison, were growing up and successfully pursuing their own university dreams. My husband, Alex, had graduated in 1995—also taking part-time courses to do so. I was the last one in my immediate family to be a university graduate.

My studies in sociology afforded me the opportunity to learn how human society functioned which I found fascinating. The study of social problems was very interesting and created an awareness in me of the need by society to develop ways of trying to ameliorate those pressing issues. I read the newspapers with that awareness focused and so developed a profound interest in those problems. While I had always been interested in politics before, now I examined the politicians' stance on these problems in Canadian society more closely. The assigned essay topics sent me to the university library where I felt very much at home having always loved reading, research and books of any kind. The research I was required to do introduced me to professional journals which I did not know existed but found extremely interesting. I usually read and took notes much more extensively than was needed. The learning process involved consumed me and frequently I lost all sense of time. I loved studying and writing reports! Preparing for exams made me anxious but only to discover what my results would be. The whole university experience met my expectations of broadening my outlook and knowledge.

And so, finally, in December of 1999, I had completed all of the requirements for my bachelor's degree. I had to wait for the Spring Convocation to actually graduate but the feeling of accomplishment gradually settled in with great satisfaction. My husband and daughters had graduated with their degrees before me and had encouraged me to enjoy this whole graduation experience to the fullest.

In May, I received a letter from the Secretary of the Senate, Ronald Smith, advising me that the Senate of Laurentian University had approved my application for graduation at the 2000 Spring Convocation ceremony.

My commencement exercises occurred on June 1, 2000 at 2:30 pm. I made an appointment with Candid Photo Studio to have my grad pictures taken. My husband had not done this and I tried to convince him to have his photo taken with me but he decided not to do so. It was a decision he regretted later. My 84 - year old father came from Wallaceburg for the auspicious day, which meant a great deal to me. My eldest daughter Jacquie drove from Toronto with her 5-year old Rachel and 2 - year old Trent. I felt elated during the convocation ceremony and couldn't wait for President Jean Watters to call my name. As I walked onto the stage my daughter yelled, "Way to go Grandma!" Everyone laughed and Dr. Watters asked me if he had heard correctly. With pleasure I told him that my family was represented by four generations at this ceremony. He then asked whether life had intervened as it had taken me so long to finish. I agreed that this was so and he congratulated me in having persevered and suggested that I probably appreciated graduating more than the twenty- somethings who were graduating with me. I agreed enthusiastically!

On Saturday, June 3, my family had organized a grand celebration for me and had invited family, many friends and neighbours to help me celebrate. I received exquisitely beautiful flowers, wonderful books and other lovely mementoes which I appreciated tremendously, but best of all was the knowledge that I had achieved a life-long dream of becoming a university graduate. I have a Bachelor of Arts, a BA! Now we are all university graduates and that's important to me.

Erna, graduate of Laurentian University, Sudbury,2000

Alex graduate of Laurentian University, 1995

ON BECOMING SIXTY

YES, IT IS a fact! This month I turned 60! It's 2001! I wonder, "How can that be?" I still feel young inside! Hopes, dreams, plans activities, still form my future. It is my firm belief that turning 60 does not signify "Old Age" as it did when I was 20. Does everyone feel this way? My hair is not yet grey—honest! Hard to deny the image in the mirror though. Wrinkles—yes-slowly, a few are appearing. It's inevitable.

Ageing is universal and unless you are summoned to your heavenly home earlier, the number of years rises inexorably. Had I noticed? At times, I must acknowledge I did. Now that I have reached that milestone the feeling of ME becoming 60 is not frightening in the least. It does, however, cause me to stop momentarily to reflect on my life thus far.

As for all of us, I believe, my life has been a roller coaster ride with the inevitable ups and downs. The important fact is that I survived them all and learned many things along the way—both from the highs and the lows. That's one momentous actuality in reaching 60, discovering that all of life is a continuous learning opportunity! Many occurrences have become cherished images in my "Box of Memories"! "My vision of life is much clearer and concrete", as someone once stated.

Working outside and inside my home, caring for my family, taking courses in the evening, eventually taking care of my ill and ageing parents caused the years to just fly by. Suddenly I realize that I have arrived at this rewarding phase of my life where there is actually time for ME! This is an unexpected bonus which I had never even contemplated. Imagine—time to become re-acquainted with the always supportive man in my life with whom I exchanged vows nearly 38 years ago. Time to enjoy my precious grandchildren. to travel, to take naps without guilt, to garden, to become more active in my church, to develop new interests, to complete projects never finished, to read to my heart's content! Time to do whatever I want—a marvellous revelation. Hey, I am now eligible to receive another monthly cheque, another bonus.

I'll also need to exercise more to maintain good health. When my 85- year old father walks better and faster than me, that is a clear message I cannot ignore.

Corresponding with close relatives and friends whether by hand - written letters or by the convenient technology of email, has always been an enjoyable experience for me. Now I will have the time to increase the frequency of contacting those who are significant to me.

Having graduated from university last year was gratifying and important.

Now that I am 60 years old, I really understand that time is to be used wisely—not wasted. Non-essential things can be freely discarded as I understand who and what are really meaningful to me. That is perhaps the most valuable lesson that the vagaries of my life have taught me.

I wonder how the next decade will broaden my life?

Life truly is a gift and an exciting adventure for which I am constantly grateful!

JOYS OF TRAVELLING

MY FIRST TRIP to Holland was with my mother for my Grandmother's funeral in 1965. That was naturally very sad but I was glad to be able to accompany Mom. Seeing my extended family again whetted my appetite to travel there and to other places as often as possible.

Alex and I have always enjoyed travelling. Sometimes we have travelled with our children and at times, it's just the two of us. Going to my homeland, Holland, I have most often travelled by myself as Alex doesn't understand Dutch and it gives me the opportunity to speak my first language freely with my extended family. He has accompanied me twice, in 1975 and 2007. I wanted my relatives to meet him and by the same token, I needed him to understand me better by learning about my roots in Hulst. He enjoyed both visits, particularly the second one in 2007 when we took a bus tour to Paris, a city he had always hoped to visit. Even though we got lost in this magnificent city, the memories are fantastic! That's a story for another day.

We have visited Florida several times especially when Alex's brother Leo and his wife Ellen lived there in a lovely gated community near Sun City Center. We spent a week with them. There was a golf course within its boundaries and indoor as well as outdoor pools. We enjoyed ourselves so much! Leo and Ellen were fantastic hosts. Alex and Leo played volleyball three mornings a week which Alex appreciated very much as he and his older brother had not spent much time together in many years. We visited Naples as well on this trip to spend some time with our beautiful niece Josanne Bundy Hill and her two sons, A.J. and Brandon. She prepared a delicious fresh salmon supper and persuaded us to spend the night. The Naples beaches are phenomenal! The next day we drove further south to Miami where we had not been before. It was interesting to see how the "other half" lives.

The Kennedy Space Center was definitely on our list and it met all of our expectations, so much so that we actually revisited there twice and left still feeling that we had not seen it all. The Spaceship Discovery was ready in the launch tower for its trip into space the following week. We were fortunate to see the spaceship in the launch tower. On our way back to Canada we detoured to Memphis, Tennessee, as we were both avid Elvis Presley fans. The line-ups to take shuttles across the road to visit his famed home, Graceland, were worth the wait. We had not realized that he and his family were buried on the grounds. The numerous gold records and his flamboyant costumes were on display in glass cases and his music played throughout the mansion. It was well-worth the visit but neither one of us felt that we needed to see it a second time.

In 2015, we spent a wonderful week in Mexico—a first for us. We had just returned from there, to fly by Porter Airlines to New York City two days later to be present for "newchoir", a Toronto mixed singing rock choir to which our daughter Jacquie belongs. They had been invited to sing at the world-famous Carnegie Hall and we did not want to miss this auspicious event to see our daughter sing there. Their performance was wonderful and the audience cheered very enthusiastically in this glorious venue. After The choir members were elated with their performance and celebrated with many of the family and friends who had travelled to see them.

Alex and I decided to spend an extra night in New York City to have a leisurely dinner and explore on our own. My husband surprised me by asking if I would like to take a carriage ride in Central Park the next day. It was lovely! It was March so there weren't any leaves on the trees affording us an excellent view of the area around the park.

For our 40th Anniversary in 2003, our daughter Allison and her husband Rey invited us to come to New Orleans where they were living at the time. We accepted readily and spent Christmas with them before our anniversary date of December 28. They showed us many interesting aspects of the "Big Easy" as this city has been referred to. The above ground cemeteries were fascinating and upon reading the inscriptions we realized that generations of families were entombed together. The brown pelicans caught my attention. They were everywhere on the banks of the Mississippi River. We visited the zoo, aquarium, a former slave plantation, Pat O'Brien's bar where we drank "hurricanes" in the French Quarter. We really got the flavour of this unique city. Two years later, in August of 2005, Hurricane Katrina destroyed the city and surrounding area. Our daughter had evacuated safely to Houston, Texas but they lost everything that they had not been able to pack into their small car. We were so relieved that they were safe and sound!! In retrospect, we knew we were so fortunate that we had experienced New Orleans before that horrific storm.

My close friend Sue called and asked if I would be interested in going on a bus pilgrimage to Europe in October of 2015. Our guides were Father Tony Man-Son-Hing and Father Trevor Scarfone, both of whom I knew. We landed at Schiphol Airport in Amsterdam. We checked in to our hotel to rest and the next morning our spiritual guides took us to a small church in the Kalverstraat where a miracle had allegedly occurred in 1345. Since the explanations were written in Dutch, I was asked to translate which I did happily. After several days in Amsterdam, we travelled on to the City of Antwerp in Belgium. Antwerp is less than 30 minutes from Hulst where I was born. When I explained to the two priests that my relatives would gladly come to see me there, they agreed. My Aunt Corrie and 7 cousins greeted me waving small Dutch flags when we arrived on the pier. What a phenomenal family afternoon we had visiting and catching up on family news! My cousin Emmy had made a reservation in a tiny restaurant nearby called, "de Boterham" which aptly translates to "The Sandwich". Many new family memories were made. Since we don't get to see each other very often this time together was precious to all of us.

Then the bus arrived and took us to Brussells, Capital of Belgium, and home of the European Union headquarters. I purchased two lovely poppy cushion covers there in an interesting indoor shopping mall. The ceilings were curved glass. We saw the huge Atomium there, a series of large balls which had been built for the 1958 World's Fair. I was particularly interested in seeing this structure as my father had promised to take me there. However, a major strike at INCO that year, prevented that from happening. In Brussells, everyone must visit "Manneke Pis", a small renowned statue of a little boy peeing. Even though I had seen it several times before, it was fun to observe it again. The real gold trim on the buildings in the city square were breath taking. On to Luxembourg where we spent the night. This journey included visits to Strasbourg, Switzerland—the Alps were amazing. Then to Milan, which had a remarkable, large church built entirely of marble sourced in the area nearby. Padua in Italy was our next stop, a university town. Venice was beautiful and very crowded as there was a marathon happening. Going to the city by gondola was a novel experience for most of us. Our final destination was Rome, a city which had been on my bucket list. St. Peter's Basilica certainly met my expectations as to its grandeur, atmosphere, and the special altar dedicated to Pope Jean Paul II. The famous Sistine Chapel painted by Michael Angelo was gorgeous. Vatican City is an independent state within the City of Rome. We spent several days in this historic city including a General Audience with Pope Francis. He came right into the crowd in St. Peter's Square in his popemobile and we saw him up close, a thrill for me. The colossal Coliseum was also visited and impressed everyone. We flew home from Rome. We had learned so much about our faith and the cities in which we were fortunate to spend time. We had celebrated Mass in chapels and churches every day. Our trip had lasted 15 days but the memories will last a lifetime.

For several winters Alex went to Florida to play golf with our good friend Floyd Laughren and Terry McKenzie. He really looked forward to these vacations. The second winter he was gone, February was extremely cold so I called my close friend, Sue Orange Nichol and begged her to find us someplace warm to vacation for two weeks. She called me back and asked me how I felt about travelling to Jamaica. That began our traditional holidays on that beautiful Caribbean island for 3 years. I really look forward to that winter break after Christmas annually. In January of 2018, we decided to take a cruise—a first for both of us. It lasted one week. We were aboard the Holland-America Line's Eurodam. We really enjoyed this experience and I would love to experience a cruise again. Neither one of us were seasick even though the seas were rough at times. The Dutch captain was Werner Timmers and I met him about the ship frequently and enjoyed speaking Dutch with him as he was very approachable. Other crew members also spoke my first language which added to my enjoyment of the voyage immensely.

Travelling is the perfect way to broaden our minds and is the best educational experience. That is why we enjoy it so much and will continue to do so as long as we are able.

Alex & Erna in Florida

A CANADIAN ADVENTURE

ON A FRIDAY night in August 2005, as we were preparing for bed at camp, my husband Alex declared that he felt like taking a long drive. Curious, I asked what he meant by, "a long drive?" "Oh", was his nonchalant reply, "I was thinking of driving through the Rockies!" My immediate reply was "I'm in the car!". Right away I emailed our friends in Edmonton and as an afterthought, Merle and Joyce Williams in Yellowknife. Joyce excited invited us to come North as well as going West.

Westward Ho! On August 25 at 5 am we left Sudbury with no reservations or exact plans as to how far we would travel each day. We prefer to travel spontaneously and let the attractions, weather or how we feel dictate our spots to spend the night. It gives a real sense of adventure to our journeys. We had our cellphone with us so that our daughters could reach us if they needed to.

Stops in the Sault, Thunder Bay and Winnipeg led us West. We stopped for a little while in Thunder Bay to admire and pay homage to Terry Fox. The diverse scenery was fascinating and never boring along Lake Superior, truly a "great lake". It was impressive to see the Sleeping Giant is a massive stone format that lays in repose watching over Thunder Bay.

Then on to Winnipeg, Manitoba where we spent the night. We stood at the famed corner of Portage & Main and realized that there was a shopping mall underneath the street. Luckily it wasn't as cold as that famed corner can be.

We entered Saskatchewan and the vast prairie landscape. We were astonished by the how the big blue sky touched the unending waving wheat fields.

Then on to Regina where we visited the interesting Royal Canadian Mounted Police Gendarmarie, a combined museum, headquarters and training facility where their world-famous Musical Ride trains. We continued on to lovely Saskatoon on a gorgeous summer Saturday where we enjoyed a Ukrainian Festival. Having so much fun, we decided to stay an extra day.

Onwards to Alberta where stops in Calgary and Edmonton followed. In St. Albert, near Edmonton, we joyfully reconnected with our dear friends Larry and Debbie Kirkpatrick as well as George and Elaine Fraser. It was here that our daughters Jacquie and Michelle called us to say New Orleans was hit by the massive Hurricane Katrina where their sister Allison lived. Allison and Rey had safely evacuated earlier to Houston, Texas. The girls gave us a phone number in Houston where Allison and Rey were temporarily staying. Immediately we turned on the TV and saw the unimaginable devastation of New Orleans wrought by the fierce winds and terrible flooding of this Category Five hurricane. We attempted numerous times to reach Allison to no avail. We contemplated turning back but knew Allison and Rey were safe in Houston.

As we proceeded towards Northern Alberta, we were awed by the beautiful scenery and felt enveloped by the huge skies. We understood the term Big Sky Country here. The Peace River valley was magnificent with a few ski hills dotting its countryside.

It is 1,700 km from Edmonton to Yellowknife in the Northwest Territories so we realized we would have long days of driving ahead of us. The first night we slept in the town of High Level, Alberta, as we had been advised to do. In the morning, we drove to the 60th Parallel, the border between Alberta and the Northwest Territories. That was exciting and we stopped to take a picture of the sign to prove that we had made it. Back into the car since we needed to drive a long distance yet to the Mackenzie River Ferry Crossing near Fort Providence. The mighty Mackenzie is well named. Although it takes only ten minutes to cross at this point by ferry, this mammoth river and the fast- flowing current caused us to comprehend the enormity of this river.

The NWT Welcome Centre was manned by a Dene gentleman who presented us with an official certificate naming us as Honourable Members of the North of Sixty Degrees Chapter Order of Arctic Adventurers. It was a great souvenir to show our family. Inside the Welcome Centre, there was a handsomely mounted Polar Bear. The man also had a wood-stove burning so that we could warm up a little. He patiently answered our many questions about what to expect as we continued our journey north. He warned us about the likelihood of large bison herds being commonly on the road. If we came upon any bison, whether a single bison or a herd to stop the car and wait until they proceeded into the forest. We would just have to be patient.

Alexandra Falls, Louise Falls and Lady Evelyn Falls were lovely dramatic surprises as we had no idea that these stunning waterfalls existed. The water coursing over the escarpments was coloured yellow due to the sandstone rock below. Pink wild roses grew in profusion all along the banks. There were excellent viewing platforms affording us spectacular views in all directions.

It was teeming rain by this time and we needed gas. We turned into a Dene reservation where we were served and the young man answered our questions. The last thirty miles or so of the road to Yellowknife was gravel he told us, we appreciated that warning. It was slower driving but finally we arrived at the home of our friends, Joyce and Merlyn Williams. We were greeted so enthusiastically. There were fantastic hosts! We learned a great deal about Yellowknife, the capital of the Northwest Territories. The home styles ranged from shacks to architectural wonders. Such contrasts! A number of people lived permanently on houseboats, moored in Great Slave Lake. One day Merlyn and Alex went for a long canoe ride on this huge lake. In winter there is an ice road across the Lake and it really reduces the travel time across the Mackenzie River to Fort Providence. The Northern Lights were magnificent, so much more brilliant that we had ever seen them before. We encountered some of the huge bison on our return journey and followed the advice we had been given to just wait for them to decide to go into the forest.

Returning to Alberta, we drove many long hours until we reached Grande Prairie where we spent the night. Then onto the Columbia Ice Fields in Jasper National Park. What a shock it was to see how much the Athabasca Glacier had receded since we last saw it in 1982. The staggering beauty of the Rockies had not diminished and are superior to the Alps in my opinion. We were once again struck by the beauty of our country.

In British Columbia we stopped at the Canyon Hot Springs and enjoyed swimming in the hot spring-fed water. Then onto Sicamous to meet my childhood friend Betty Makala-Durocher and her husband Rollie. Sicamous is called the "Houseboat" capital of Canada and our friends and their family enjoyed vacationing in this manner. Peachland was our next destination, the home of my nephew Paul de Burger and his beautiful wife Angela. They had received an email from Michelle emphasizing that Rey and Allison were safe and on their way back to Ontario. Penticton is short distance away and off we went to visit Alex's sister Marie Claire or M.C. as she prefers and her hospitable husband Dave. We stayed in that picturesque town for a few days and every day M.C. and Dave showed us a different winery. Our favourite was the Mission Hill winery, situated on top of a hill offering a stunning view of the Okanagan Valley. The amazing wine country was impressive and very enjoyable. The grapes were ripe and it was interesting to see them hanging from the vines.

Vancouver was our next destination, one of Canada's premiere tourist destinations. The immense trees in Stanley Park amazed us. We explored the city for a couple of days then drove to Twawwassen Terminal to take the ferry to Vancouver Island.

In Victoria, we met our nephew Emile Delongchamp. His dad, Johnny, lived in the picturesque town of Duncan, a place which has the most astonishing murals on many of the buildings. It was good to see Johnny whose wife Lucille, Alex's sister, had sadly died several years previously. We continued on to Canada's only rain forest which was absolutely breathtaking. Then to our final destination, Tofino which is the Pacific terminus of the Trans Canada highway. The Pacific Ocean and beaches were unbelievably gorgeous and we enjoyed a stunning sunset over the ocean. We removed our shoes to wade in the Pacific Ocean, something that we had never expected to experience. A nearby beach, called Long Beach, had signs warning everyone of dangerous currents. There were surfers catching waves, regardless of the warning signs posted. We drove to Victoria to see the astonishing Butchart Gardens which were constructed in an old quarry. Hard to believe!

Back to the mainland via the ferry to begin our trek home. We took a detour to Drumheller, in the Canadian Badlands of Alberta. The voodoos have to be seen to understand the power of the years of erosion. Our breath was taken away by the shear size and shapes of them. This area is world famous for its deposits of dinosaur bones. A visit to the Royal Tyrell Museum was worthwhile and gave us a better understanding of these huge beasts, so long extinct.

We decided to drive home via the United States for a different route going east. Minnesota provided us with an unexpected revelation. As we were driving, I noticed a sign stating "Headwaters of the Mississippi". The mighty Mississippi River, which flows down to the Gulf of Mexico and through New Orleans, has its' source in Itasca State Park. It was a small stream just 18 inches deep! At its mouth it is a thousand feet wide and two hundred feet deep.

Our trip had taken a full month. Our varied and engrossing experiences across Canada had given us numerous memories to enjoy for a long time.

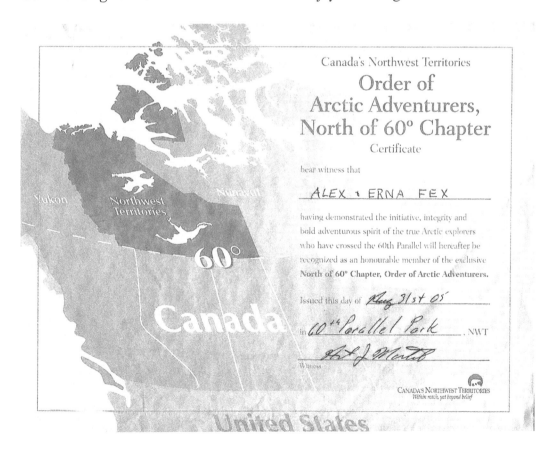

LOST IN PARIS

FINALLY, THE DAY arrived! Alex and I were going to Paris with a guided bus trip from my hometown of Hulst in The Netherlands. It was in May of 2007. We had no difficulty rising at 5 am! Tante Corrie drove us to the bus stop. After putting our luggage in the compartment under the bus, we were on our way. Both of us were excited as we had been looking forward to this for a long time. We settled in for the four-hour ride. Every seat was occupied for this trip as it was the first bus voyage of the season. Our guide began to explain what we would see and do, while travelling through Belgium, a short distance from Hulst.

Halfway to our destination the bus stopped for a coffee break. We discovered that our guide spoke no English so I had to translate everything he said for Alex. That was difficult for me. We had been given to understand that he would give his information in Dutch, English, French and German.

As we approached the city limits of this vibrant, historic city, the feeling of anticipation intensified. It was palpable and the level of conversation also rose. The ring road was negotiated successfully by our experienced chauffeur. The volume of traffic heading into the city's core was expected but still remarkable. The bus driver parked on a side street of the famed Champs Elysees and we were given our first taste of freedom in this magnificent city. We explored the area nearby, the Place de la Concorde, the beautiful Jardin des Plantes and even climbed to the top of a nearby building which afforded us a spectacular vista of this tourist mecca. The Eiffel Tower was an excellent point of reference for locating other important sites.

At the appointed time, we returned to our bus now anxious to get to the hotel to prepare for dinner at a nearby restaurant.

Not having stayed in European hotels before we were unprepared for how small our room was. The double bed took up nearly all the floor space. We had a tiny bathroom consisting of a toilet, small sink, and shower. The floor to ceiling windows gave us a great view of the streets near the Athene Hotel on Magenta Boulevard. Traffic sounds were unceasing. Alex and I were elated to be in Paris!

We gathered for dinner at a small French restaurant nearby. The food was somewhat disappointing but the meal gave us the chance to become acquainted with our fellow travellers. A delicious red wine accompanied our meal. An accordionist wearing a beret had been hired for our entertainment which I really enjoyed.

After dinner, our guide led us to the exquisite, white Sacre Coeur Basilica located on top of the Butte Monmartre in Paris. This is the highest place in Paris. We walked for nearly an hour constantly ascending steps, narrow streets and alleyways. However, when we reached the top, the view of the rooftops with their many small chimneys was most interesting. Gazing down over the city of Paris, the view from the steps of Sacre Coeur was breath-taking! We entered the church to find Mass going on as it always is 24 hours a day. We were impressed by the number of young people attending Mass at 11 pm. We lit candles in memory of our deceased mothers. Then it was time to leave and meet up with our guide and our bus companions.

We started to walk down the hill towards the Place de Tertre where painters were working and the cafes were busy with revellers. Loud music and talk surrounded us and we found it intoxicating. To me this was "le vrai Paris" as I had imagined it. We entered a small gallerie to purchase some prints and postcards. Suddenly we realized we needed to find our group to return to the hotel. They were nowhere to be seen. At this point we were not yet panicking thinking that since we had come up this hill we would descend and catch up. However, this was not to be.

We walked and walked down the narrow dark streets having no idea where we would end up. We soon realized that we were lost! By this time, I was so exhausted that I flopped down on a chair outside a small café. The waiter came out to ask if he could help me. My enfeebled reply to him was, "On est perdu!" My husband was attempting to figure out our location by looking at his street map under the dim light of a street lantern. The young man brought me some water and proceeded to explain to Alex how to get to a main artery. Good thing we spoke French! We followed his directions and continued walking. Then I panicked and became hysterical. Alex grabbed me by the arm and asserted, "Erna, we're lost. Who would you rather be lost with in Paris than me?" He succeeded in bringing me to my senses and I regained some self-control. We began to look at our situation as an adventure. We continued walking, descending the whole time. At one point we came upon a small group of young men playing jacks. That scared me a little but they were oblivious to us and we continued safely on our way down.

Finally, in the distance we saw lights. We were very excited! We came out at the Boulevard de Rochefort, in the red-light district of Paris. (We didn't know that until someone told us so later!) The famed Moulin Rouge night club is located there and it even crossed my mind for a moment to have a look inside the lobby. Alex couldn't believe it! Instead we noticed a Metropolitaine sign and decided to see if we could figure out how to get back to our hotel. We were at the Blanche stop and noticed Boulevard Magenta on the map, where our hotel was located. Down we went into the bowels of the old subway. Checking the ubiquitous maps again, Alex realized which train we needed to take and where we had to change trains to go east. We debarked at Gare Est, a huge train station which we had noticed on the way to our hotel. As we left that station, we noticed a "Burger King" fast food restaurant and I recalled seeing it close to our hotel. From there we walked to the hotel quite easily and surprised our guide and others. What a relief! We joined them in a glass of wine explaining how we had found our way back. The guide was somewhat uncomfortable as he knew he should never have left without us.

Thankfully, we were safe and had a new interesting story to relate to our friends and family.

Sacre Coeur Basilica

Sisters

"A SISTER CAN be your conscience, your confidante, your champion." (Anon)

Sisters are really gifts that keep on giving. My three sisters are all incredible to me in their own way. My baby sister Marianne was a very special birthday present when I turned eleven. I already had three brothers, but this was my first little sister! I was ecstatic! The fact that she was born with multiple physical and mental disabilities did not lessen my love for her and made her even more appreciated. Every day when we came home from Creighton Mine Public School, as soon as we had greeted our Mom, we all automatically surrounded Marianne's bassinet for our baby's lovely smile. Her vivid blue eyes and beautiful red curly hair entranced us. Unfortunately, Marianne died when she was nearly one year old. In that one short year she drew our family extremely close together although she was not aware of that, of course. That was her exceptional gift to us.

My sister Mary Alice, known as Liesje, was born shortly after we lost Marianne. She was healthy and we were enchanted watching her growth and development. With her we could do fun activities which had been impossible with Marianne. When she was a little older, she slept with me in our double bed for many years, which I loved. So many questions! It was never boring! Liesje did well in school and continued her studies after she was married and her sons had been born until she achieved her Masters Degree in English. I was so very proud of her! She is an excellent mother to Kerry and Patrick and they appreciate their Mom. Now that she is a grandmother as well, she enjoys her grandchildren fully. Liesje and I have similar tastes in clothes and have several times purchased the same item although we live hundreds of kilometers apart.

Seven years later another beautiful, healthy, little sister was born just six weeks after our brother Willy had been killed. She was named Lillian after my sister-in-law Lillian Fex. Lillian had dark hair when she was born– a first in our family. I was almost 19. Our parents asked my brother Ron and me to be her godparents. Lilly became our doll as we were all so much older. We enjoyed watching her grow and undoubtedly spoiled her. Her pretty hair became blond and it was soon evident that she would be taller than Liesje and me. Lillian clung to me at our wedding reception. We noticed that when we developed our pictures. Lillian and Liesje performed their duties well. Both of my little sisters spent a great deal of time with us and I loved that they enjoyed coming so often.

My parents and sisters moved to Wallaceburg in 1969 when Liesje was sixteen and Lillian was nine. Although we now lived far away from each other, the loving feelings we had for each other were not affected at all. We have always enjoyed spending time together in spite of the age differences and the distance between us.

Lillian was an involved and loving mother to Joshua and identical twin daughters, Mallory and Kaleena. She was a very busy Mom! Now that she has four beautiful grandchildren, and a new grandson, she has entered a most enjoyable phase of her life as "Nana". Lillian was an exceptional primary caregiver to our parents, Alice and Florent, in their later years. We appreciated that very much as the rest of us lived far away. I travelled to Wallaceburg frequently to give her a break. It also gave us sister-time which I loved. Being her godmother, we always felt a special bond.

I thank my parents daily for giving me such wonderful, unique and caring sisters.

Alex and I have 3 lovely, intelligent daughters, Jacquie, Michelle and Allison. We are very proud of the parents they are and of their productive lives as well as of the spouses they chose.

Three Fex sisters Jacquie, Allison and Michelle

June 2007 –
An Eventful Month

ON FRIDAY JUNE 15, 2007 my sister Lillian called from Wallaceburg to inform me that our Dad was being sent to hospital by handi-transit for some tests. At his age of 91 this was not an unusual occurrence so I was not unduly concerned. I asked her to keep me informed and told my husband to go ahead and play golf in his tournament as he had been planning and looking forward to doing. Off he went. Lillian called again a short time later with a tone of voice in which I heard concern immediately. "The nursing home just called to say that they were sending Dad to the Wallaceburg Hospital by ambulance as he was unresponsive and his face had caved in." What did that mean? I became worried and asked her to keep me informed as she promised to do.

When I had not heard anything by early afternoon, I decided to call the hospital myself directly, assuming that our Dad had been admitted. When I identified myself, I was told that this was indeed the case and was put through to the nursing station on the second floor. I asked the attending nurse how my Dad was doing and her reply was "poorly". That naturally shocked me and I requested further details. She began to tell me that his kidneys were failing, he was unresponsive, short of breath, and in general was not doing well. In my head I knew where this was leading but in denial, I asked her if we needed to come to Wallaceburg immediately. She asked me where I lived and when I replied Sudbury, wanted to know how long it would take us to get there. My reply, "seven hours at least." She suggested we leave immediately.

Suddenly, I burst into tears. I called my brother Frank who also lives in Sudbury to tell him the terrible news. He and his partner Karen prepared to leave as soon as they could. Calling Alex on his cell phone on the golf course was my next action. Packing my suitcase and pulling some of his clothes out of his closet kept me occupied most of the time until he returned home. Of course, he didn't come quickly enough in my distressed state. By the time we stopped for gas and oil, I was really in a state of conflicting emotions. Worry, fear, anger that it took us so long to get underway, all added up to a person who was not amenable to ordinary conversation! We still had a seven- hour drive ahead of us! My husband is a very calm person—the perfect foil to excitable me. He assured me that he would get me there as quickly as possible and we were on our way. Alex has known my Dad for 48 years and he cared a great deal about him and I knew that.

The drive seemed unending! I wanted so much to get to the hospital before my wonderful Dad passed away! By now I realized that this was inevitable although some tiny part of me kept hoping that this was not so. Even though Dad was 91 ½ years old, I was not yet ready to let go. He had not been ill at all for a long time. Could his life end so suddenly? When we were getting closer to Wallaceburg, I called my brother's cell phone asking in a frightened voice, "Is Dad still alive?" "No, Erna," was his gentle reply. "He died at 10:20—a half hour ago." I asked Frank not to allow the hospital staff to remove Dad from his bed until I arrived. I felt the loss instantly but urged Alex to speed up. I needed to see my father as soon as possible.

When we reached the hospital, I jumped out of the car with Alex calling after me that running at this point would make no difference. Of course, I paid no attention—I HAD to see my Dad! When we reached his room, my brother Frank came right over to me to hug me as did my sister Lillian. They let me go so I could actually envelop my Dad in my arms as I needed to do. He hardly looked like the Dad I remembered as his face had indeed caved in. His hair was still black on top and I absentmindedly rubbed it constantly while my brother and my sister were telling me all about his final hours. I needed to know every small detail. Frank told me that Dad had sat up just before he passed away, looked around the room, then lay down and took his last few breaths. Frank was holding his hand. As far as they could tell he was not suffering any pain. That last bit of information was most important to me as I was always concerned that he not be in pain. Whenever I visited him it was always a question I asked him. His answer was no every time.

After some time had elapsed, we all went to my sister Lillian's home. Most of the night was spent in reminiscing about our father.

In the morning we had to phone our sister Liesje in Oshawa and our sister-in-law Frances in Oakville so that she could contact our brother Ron who was in Vancouver at a conference. Then the phone calls to other family members and to our relatives in Holland who were understandably shocked with the suddenness of Dad's death. Alex and I had been in Holland with them in May when we were questioned constantly about Dad's health and living conditions. They were pleased to hear that he was happy and in good health.

Later Frank, Lillian and I went to Nicholl's Funeral Home to make the arrangements. I asked the Funeral Director to puff up Dad's face as he had always had a lovely round face. He promised to do his best. Since the funeral was pre-arranged most decisions had been made. We brought his clothes and the obituary which I had written. Then we had another difficult task to perform. We drove to Fairfield Park Long Term Care Facility which we had referred to as the nursing home, to empty Dad's room. We gave my father's lazy-boy chair to his room-mate. As we were leaving, Frank remarked, "Here we have what is left of his whole life in a few cardboard boxes". A poignant comment. Daryl, my sister's fiancé, had prepared a wonderful meal for the entire family which we enjoyed immensely.

The next day was Sunday—Father's Day. The homily at Mass was all about honouring our dads and showing them how much we loved them. My sister and I lost it and both of us cried our eyes out. Father Greg came down from the altar to hug and comfort us in our grief. We both appreciated that very much.

Our daughter Allison, her husband Rey and baby son Matthieu drove from Toronto to Wallaceburg to be with us that afternoon and to show support to me and other family members who were arriving. I appreciated that so much! Our little grandson as well as my niece Kaleena's baby Dylan, were wonderful distractions! It was an extremely hot day and we spent our time outside until evening when Alex and I retired to our air - conditioned hotel room. It was there that I began to write my memories of my Dad as that is how I deal best with stressful moments in my life. Losing my Dad was certainly that! We had decided that because of Dad's advanced age we would only have visitation for two hours on Monday evening. All five surviving children were able to be present, as were ten of the twelve grandchildren and six of the eight great-grandchildren. That was truly a blessing! He would have been very pleased! Alex had typed up the selection of my memories and after the prayers I read my efforts which elicited understanding nods and smiles from my family.

The funeral took place on Tuesday June 19, at 11 am from Our Lady Help of Christians Church, which had been our parents' church all the years they lived in Wallaceburg. Grandchildren were pall bearers, and other family members participated in the liturgy by doing readings, carrying flowers, and bringing the offerings to the priest, making it a most meaningful funeral mass. Our brother Ron gave a wonderful eulogy connecting world history events with our father's long life-span. This really emphasized just how long Dad had lived and the immense historical changes which had occurred during his 91 ½ years! Our Father was then taken to Riverview Cemetery in Wallaceburg where he was buried beside our mother Alice who had died ten years previously in 1997. It was raining by then which perfectly matched our mood of sorrow. It was difficult to walk away from the gravesite knowing that now both of our parents were gone.

My sister Liesje's husband Bert DeJeet had not been able to attend Dad's funeral as he was himself in hospital in Oshawa suffering from inoperable lung cancer. Bert's prognosis was very poor and it had been predicted that his time was limited. Liesje called Bert often from Wallaceburg and he asked her to express his condolences to the rest of us. That was typical of thoughtful Bert! Consequently, after the reception, Liesje and her sons Patrick and Kerry and daughter—in—law Kathy, left to return to Oshawa to be at Bert's bedside. Within the next several days things went very wrong with Bert and so on Saturday morning to our shocked surprise, Liesje called to say that Bert had been taken off life support. How could that be? He had always been such a vibrant active man—full of life and a wonderful husband to my sister! Everyone loved him. On Monday June 25, Bert died—just ten days after our Dad, and exactly three weeks since he was diagnosed. Bert was 67. His death really had a profound effect on Alex and me as he was almost the same age as we are. If we needed another reminder of our mortality, that was it!

Bert's Memorial Service on Friday June 29, was fittingly held at Durham College in Oshawa where he and Liesje had met and where both had taught. It was a wonderful tribute to a most deserving man. His two children and grand-children attended. Hundreds of people filled the room—colleagues, friends, family, Oshawa's Mayor, members of the police force. We will miss him very much! Bert's ashes were lovingly spread at his favourite fishing hole near his beloved cottage, as he had wished.

Because Bert was a member of the Durham Region's Police Services Board, town flags were flown at half mast throughout the region in his honour. A fitting tribute indeed.

In the midst of all this grief, there was a ray of sunshine when my sister Lillian married her dear Daryl. The wedding had been planned long before the sad events that overtook us but it was lovely to be together to celebrate how life moves forward.

Dad (Florent de Burger)

RETROSPECTIVE ON OUR 45TH ANNIVERSARY – 2008

In September of 1963, when Alex proposed to me at my parents' home in Whitefish, no thought of the distant future crossed our minds. It was the immediate present which concerned us totally. Happiness infused every part of me as I enthusiastically said "YES!" We excitedly informed my parents who were not really surprised. We had been dating for more than four years.

So, on a sparkly, cold, winter day, December 28, 1963, we were married in St. Christopher's Catholic Church in Whitefish with our entire future ahead of us. After our afternoon reception at Creighton Mine's Cabrini Hall, we travelled to Montreal by train for our honeymoon. Upon our return we settled into married life at Carbone's Apartment in Creighton Mine located directly across the street from Creighton Mine Public School where I was teaching. The children had to adjust to their teacher's new name as I of course insisted they call me Mrs. Fex instead of Miss de Burger. I was very proud of my new status. Both Alex and I were quite young—just 22 years old, and with the naïveté of youth saw only moonlight and roses ahead of us.

Inevitably, problems were encountered—some serious, but with compromise and hard work we managed to conquer them and learn from the difficulties. These caused us to re-evaluate and adjust our relationship numerous times over the decades. As humourist author the late Erma Bombeck said, "Life is not a bowl of cherries".

In 1965 we were given the opportunity to rent a "company house" from INCO which was most fortunate for us and our baby girl Jacqueline. We loved living on Wavell Street in Creighton! We had excellent neighbours who really cared about each other. Our children were everyone's children and as they were playing outside, all looked out for them. Our second daughter, Michelle, was born while we lived there and we joyfully introduced her to our neighbours. We were part of the community and both Alex and I loved that!

In 1972, we purchased our first house at 27 Moxam Drive in Waters. Loath as we were to leave Creighton Mine the time had come to embark on the home-owning facet of our lives. Bringing our third baby, Allison, from the hospital to this house made it truly a home to us. We were fortunate to have three healthy little girls and felt blessed indeed. Our family was now complete and each birth had brought Alex and me closer together. The responsibility of raising these three girls was a continual challenge and we did our best to bring them up to become active, contributing members of society. We did not always agree on how to approach the tests continually facing us but with discussion, compromises at times, our daughters have become wonderful productive adults of whom we are very proud. They are also conscientious parents to our five grandchildren whom we cherish!

When our eldest daughter, Jacquie, decided to attend Trent University in Peterborough in 1983, she was the first to leave the nest and while we missed her dreadfully, we recognised that yet another phase of our lives had just begun. We were the parents of a university student! After four years, in 1987, now we were the parents of a university graduate! Life was moving so very quickly it seemed.

In 1988, a very beautiful chapter of our lives began with the birth of our first grandchild, Emily, daughter of Michelle. Instantly this gorgeous baby girl became the light of our lives! Michelle and Emily spent a great deal of time with us which we loved as we watched her discover and experience new things daily. Alex and I were totally captivated by our Em. Four more amazing grandchildren followed—Rachel, Trent, Matthieu and Nicholas—all of whom have been brought to camp to experience and revel in this unique Northern experience. Alex and I eagerly anticipated and relished each visit. Each is unique with their own talents and interests which makes them so special.

Our camp (it's camp, not cottage) at French River, purchased in 1977, was, and is - a special family place and spending time there with our daughters and grandchildren was most precious. Alex and I were always able to leave whatever problems we might be facing at the time behind us while we were there. But also, at other stressful occasions, we discovered it to be the perfect spot to try to find solutions to our difficulties by having the time to discuss, without distractions, what our next step would be. This camp which we had purchased in 1977 was and still is—our haven, for so many reasons. We have never allowed a TV to be brought in as that was totally unnecessary. It encouraged our children and later our grandchildren to seek other amusements. Board games, cards, reading, Dutch shuffleboard and of course outdoor fun such as fishing, swimming and campfires—not to mention catching frogs, passed the time at camp with much enjoyment for all. Who needs a TV?

The time had come to sell our four - bedroom house and move into Sudbury. Yes, it was difficult especially for me, but it was a mutual decision as such a huge change in our lives had to be. We are presently living in a spacious apartment in Sudbury which now feels like home to me. It took me three years to fully appreciate our new surroundings with Alex showing much consideration for my feelings. He loved it from Day One. Our daughter Michelle and her partner Mark also lived in that co-op. Then our granddaughter Emily and her partner Joe Robidoux moved into the same co-op as well. In November 2009, they presented us with our first great grandchild, Aayden Alexander making us great grandparents unbelievably. We feel so blessed to know and enjoy this little boy.

We began travelling more together; to New Orleans in 2003, Western and Northern Canada in 2005, to Europe in 2007, Quebec City and Florida in 2008. We found this to be stimulating, educational and the most wonderful of shared experiences. We relaxed on our trips and thoroughly enjoyed each other's company even after many hours spent daily in the car. Enjoying the same radio programs made the journeys most entertaining. The trip to Louisiana in 2003 had three purposes - to visit our daughter Allison and son-in-law Rey who lived in New Orleans and also to celebrate Christmas and our 40th Anniversary while we were there. It was perfect!

Now we have reached our 45th Anniversary and Alex presented me with a lovely sapphire ring to mark the occasion. Fortunately, we are both in good health and able to enjoy many activities together and separately. At age 67 we are at a mutually satisfying stage of our lives with deep understanding of each other's needs and wants. Our love for each other is profound and we feel closer to each other every day. We realise that we are blessed. Life is indeed very good!

Alex & Erna – 45th Anniversary.

The Summer of 2010

ALTHOUGH THE WEATHER was hot and sunny, the summer of 2010 turned out to be a difficult one for us.

It started the evening of June 30 when I tripped down some stairs and fell forcefully against the opposite wall. This resulted in a great deal of blood everywhere, in our hallway, on me, the mats—and frighteningly it kept flowing. I felt pain everywhere especially in my face. That in itself was scary! Am I vain? I don't think so but my face is always the first thing anyone sees when we meet. I managed to crawl to Alex's office to call my daughter, then my granddaughter who also lives close by, but was unable to reach either one. Then I tried to reach Alex on his blackberry again. Thankfully he answered this time. "Alex, come home quickly, I fell and there is blood everywhere!" He was home in a very few minutes, entered the house and could not believe what he saw. There literally was blood all over. He reached down and raised me to my shaky feet wondering aloud where all this blood was coming from.

Quickly my husband gave me a towel to put in front of my face. Then off to the ER at Sudbury Regional Hospital. Fortunately, it was not busy at 9:45 that evening and I was called to triage quite soon after our arrival. The nurse gave me pads of gauze but I soon realized that my soiled towel was much more useful in staunching the blood which was still flowing steadily from my nose and mouth. Shortly after, I was called to the back area and asked to wait there until a room was available for me. I asked if my husband could join me there and very reluctantly the nurse gave him permission to do so as it was not busy. When we were moved to an examination room, we knew that we were making progress. Soon ER Doctor Kusnierczyk came in to examine me. His comments were disconcerting to say the least. When I told him that both of my hands were very painful, he sent me for x-rays of my hands as well as my nose. Back to the examination room where he showed us the developed photos. My hands showed no fractures but he pointed out to me that my nose was broken. That astounded me as that possibility had never crossed my mind.

The injuries inside my mouth were sutured requiring three stitches inside my mouth, three on my bottom lip and three more on top of my nose. Home we went and dropped into bed, both of us exhausted as it was 3:30 am by this time. The next morning, I was still in a great deal of pain in my face but not in my hands although my right hand had very little strength in it. Looking in the mirror was very traumatic for me as my entire face was bruised and swollen along with the sutures on my nose and lower lip. It was horrible and made me cry. It was impossible to eat due to the stitches inside my lower lip.

The ER doctor had made an appointment for me that next Tuesday with a cosmetic surgeon, Dr. Hendel, in case I required some work on my face. Thankfully I did not, however when I told him about my weak right hand, he examined it and told me that my wrist was sprained. He ordered a splint be put on the wrist. In reality it was like a half cast which I could remove for showers. He also ordered physiotherapy for several weeks which helped to strengthen my wrist totally.

We did have one bright special day on July 10. Our great grandson Aayden Robidoux, was baptized in Val Caron and the ceremony was beautiful, meaningful and very emotional especially for Alex and me—his great grandparents. Who knew we would ever be able to experience knowing and loving the next generation in our family? The joy all of us present felt, was palpable. All of our family, including our five grandchildren, were there and a wonderful celebration was hosted by Joe's parents, Pauline and Greg Robidoux.

On August 1, we received a call from Alex's sister Denise informing us that her son-in-law Marc Cyr had died of a sudden heart attack in Afghanistan. Marc was only 49 years old. What a shock! Our 42- year- old niece Leanne was devastated to be a widow so young. It took 14 days for Marc's body to be returned by the military to Ottawa from Afghanistan. Marc was a veteran but had been asked to return to fulfill a contract using his skill set. We drove to Ottawa to support our niece who is also our godchild. Her appearance was shocking, her hugs were tight and long-lasting with all of us shedding tears.

At the funeral home military personnel were present as well as family and friends of both Marc and Leanne as well as their children Kassandra and Alex. The Masons did a lovely compassionate memorial service for Marc in the funeral home chapel. It was a rainy day which suited our feelings and the occasion perfectly. The next morning, a warm sunny day, we gathered at a beautiful little church for the funeral which was very sad. Watching the hearse drive away with the casket was heart-wrenching especially for Leanne and the children as well as Marc's mother and sisters. We returned to Sudbury after the reception.

Just 2 weeks after that funeral we learned that Alex's brother Ronald had passed away. Ron was 70 and had been ill for a long time but we had not expected his death so soon. We went to Pioneer Manor where he had resided for the past 9 years and met his wife Claudette and daughter Mae and her husband Ian there, as well as some of his siblings. We were plunged into grief again. The Memorial Mass at Our Lady of Hope was attended by the family as well as many cousins. Alex and I were grateful that most of our family were able to be there as well. The choir sang beautifully adding to the loveliness of the ceremonies presided over by Father Larry Rymes, our parish priest.

On October 3, our sister-in-law Ellen called from Barrie to inform us that Leo, Alex's older brother, had been admitted to the Royal Victoria Hospital and she wasn't sure what the cause was. After many tests it was determined that the diagnosis was osteosarcoma—bone cancer, the same cancer that had claimed the life of Terry Fox. This wonderful man survived this battle but died a few years later causing Alex and and our entire family enormous grief.

The bad news continued—now on the de Burger side. My sister Lillian, the youngest in our family of seven, called on October 25 to tell me that she has been having mini strokes since 2007. Lillian had just turned 50. Understandably she was very upset and frightened. It hit me too. The diagnosis explains many things that have been happening for quite some time. She has been dealing with headaches, memory loss, weakness, shaking, blacking out—perhaps even her recurring bouts of depression. As well as being my sister, Lillian is my goddaughter and has always been close to me. Since our mother became terminally ill in 1992 and later died in 1997, I have been her confidant. Lillian is doing better but that summer was a very scary one for our family on both sides.

GOLDEN ANNIVERSARY
1963 — 2013

DECEMBER 28, 2013 dawned as a cold, windy day. As soon as I woke up, I realized joyfully that this was the day of our 50th Wedding Anniversary—our Golden Anniversary. Our entire family would be present with us in Sudbury for this important day in our marriage and in our family. That was the most important part for both of us. Our three daughters, Jacquie, Michelle and Allison along with their spouses, Scott, Mark and Rey, would all be with us. Naturally the presence of our grandkids, Emily, Rachel, Trent, Matthieu and Nicholas and our great grandson Aayden, would make the day perfect!

I had reserved the Party Room at Carlin Co-op where we were living then, as a cousin, Rosie Fex, was coming to photograph our family to mark the occasion. The pictures were beautiful and we were all very happy with them. Rosie took her time and took photos of various groupings and single families. She was patient and knew just what to say to our younger grandchildren to get the poses she wanted. The one exception was our 4-year-old great grandson Aayden. He was not having his picture taken and that was all there was to it. Rosie managed to snap some pictures of him and his Mom, Emily, unobtrusively. We also wanted some photos of our four generations composed of Great Grandmother Erna, Grandmother Michelle, Mother Emily and Aayden. No better luck with him with those either. Rosie photographed Alex and I up close and I love that picture.

Alex had made reservations at a lovely restaurant, Mr. Prime Rib, for the whole family. It was so fantastic for the two of us to be surrounded by all of our children, their spouses and all of our grandchildren that evening.

From the family of Jacquie, Scott, Rachel and Trent we received a special photobook compiled by Jacquie. We appreciated all of the time she had spent finding and labelling the photos. It truly is a phenomenal treasure which we enjoy perusing over and over again.

We had decided to have a celebration for family and friends in the Spring due to possible unsafe road conditions in winter in Northern Ontario. Subsequently, we reserved a large room at the Northbury Hotel for our party on April 26, 2014. It was a lovely sunny day. Alex and I canvassed several stores before we found enough tulips for all the round tables which had been set up for us. I needed to have tulips, my favourite flowers, for this day. I brought wedding and family pictures to set on each table as well, to interest our guests. Our daughter Jacquie and her family decorated the room beautifully. About 70 friends and family came to join us in celebrating our Golden Anniversary. We received flowers and many generous gifts.

Our long-time friend, Judy Corletto, came from Cambridge and I was very happy to spend some time with her. Creightonite friends Donald and Shirley Brown made the trip from North Bay which we appreciated. Our friend Ed Tyreman journeyed from Sault Ste. Marie and met many mutual friends whom he had known in Lively. That group was reminiscing and laughing the whole time. It was so great to observe them having such a good time. Every member of my Memoirs group and their spouses attended to celebrate with us and our family. This group has become very close to me and I was very glad that they were able to be present for this happy occasion in our lives.

The cake from Regency Bakery was beautiful and delicious and I had brought the original wedding cake topper from 50 years ago and placed it on the cake. I was happy that I had saved it. Our daughter Jacquie and her husband Scott had borrowed it for their wedding cake in 1992 and that made me happy. Celebrating a Golden Anniversary is not possible for everyone. We feel blessed that we were able to do so and are in good health to enjoy it.

This was indeed a fabulous stage of our lives—a time to feel blessed as we anticipated many more anniversary celebrations.

Erna & Alex

Alex & Erna & Daughters

Whole family (13 people)

MY FATHER'S HANDS

AFTER RECEIVING A delightful email entitled, "Grandma's Hands", I envisioned my father's hands, a natural enough connection considering my father's venerable age of 92 at his death in June of 2007. When I visited Dad, he would sometimes silently stare at his hands while he was deep in thought. I would ask him what he was seeing in his mind's eye and he would smile at me and usually say, "Oh, nothing!" By gently questioning him he might start to talk about some aspect of his early life. Knowing my father's life story, I understand the many tasks his hands had accomplished. His mother Julia first held his baby hands lovingly in her own. Farm chores were done as a child with his father and four brothers without ever a complaint. Those hands peeled buckets of potatoes for his stepmother Philomena, as she was frail after the birth of his sister Maria. Playing cards with his father and brothers and later with friends, was a pastime he enjoyed all his life. His hands gathered potatoes from the fields and apples from the orchard. My father's hands milked cows and lovingly caressed and brushed his beloved horses.

When he broke his right elbow in an unfortunate farm accident, he wrote notes to family in Holland with his left hand informing them of the birth of Baby Marianne. When our mother had gone to visit her family in Holland in 1956, he wrote her long letters keeping her up to date about the rest of us at home. While living in Creighton Mine he became an expert blueberry picker and his hands were blue from the juice of those tasty berries. He crafted lids for the filled baskets and carried them to the Creighton Mine train station on his way to work. The family earned some extra money from the berries which was welcome and necessary.

My father's hands became miner's hands while he worked deep underground at No.5 Shaft at Creighton Mine. After a serious heart attack, he bought a bicycle for exercise and those hands gripped the handlebars for many hours. A storekeeper at various times in his life saw his hands placing items on store shelves and using the cash register.

His hands embraced his beloved wife Alice for 56 years. He held each one of his seven children at birth and throughout our lives. The "heaviest burden he ever carried"—his words - was his one- year old baby daughter Marianne after she died in Creighton Mine in 1953, to take her little body to the funeral home. With his hands he comforted his 15 year -old son Willy as he was dying in 1960 after a terrible car accident.

With those same hands he shook colleagues' hands to seal a deal—his word as good as any document. Dirt under his fingernails indicated that he had been transplanting plants in the little greenhouse he built in Creighton. "Clean dirt" is how he would refer to that. A hot cup of coffee was always satisfying to him.

My father loved to read and instilled that love in me and my siblings and so many books passed through his hands even though English was his second language. He had an intense interest in politics, sports and world affairs and read the news magazine Maclean's from cover to cover for many years. Newspapers were eagerly awaited each day for the same reason. Prayer books also rested in his hands as he was deeply faithful to his Catholicism. Rosary beads slipped through his hands often as he prayed silently and unobtrusively. Shooting pool was a life long pastime which developed when he was a teenager in Holland. Dad became an excellent archer also at that time—a passion he was able to enjoy again when he and Mom moved to Wallaceburg in 1969. He was very competitive participating in international shoots in Detroit and other places in Michigan and won many trophies. Only the best compound bow would do for his experienced hands. His grandchildren benefited from his expertise as he taught them his beloved sport in Wallaceburg. It was a wonderful way for him to bond with them. He was even asked to teach archery at the local high school and his picture appeared in the local newspaper. My father's hands were very strong. But also, those hands became gentle and protective when he was holding a new grandchild or great grandchild. I will never forget the sight of my father lovingly holding my mother's hands as she lay dying.

My father's hands were those of a son, brother, husband, father, father-in-law, uncle, grandfather and great grandfather. They defined the many roles he had in his long and productive life. I miss those hands and always will.

A Health Scare

I HAVE ALWAYS been a firm believer in getting my mammograms every 2 years. So on Tuesday February 18, 2014, I went to the Sudbury Breast Clinic at the Out Patient Centre (formerly called Memorial Hospital) for my mammogram as usual. When I left the Clinic to come home and thought, "Well that's done for another 2 years."

To my astonishment on Wednesday February the 19, I received a call from the Clinic telling me I must return there the very next day. That was strange to me as I have never been called back before. Of course, my mind was imagining numerous scenarios as to what this could mean.

After a short wait the technician did my second mammogram and it seemed to me that it was more intense, but perhaps not. She took the x-rays to the radiologist check them who then ordered an ultra sound to be done immediately. Again, this was very unusual to me. I didn't even know that such a test was done at the Clinic as part of a breast examination. I was advised to call my family physician and make appointment with him the following week to get the results.

So, Alex and I went to the Lively Medical Centre on Tuesday, February 25. Our long-time family physician Dr. Peter Bayly met with us. He had received the mammogram results but not the results of the ultra sound. His assistant began calling the Breast Clinic to obtain that and have it faxed to his office. We waited nearly an hour and then the assistant handed the doctor the sheet.

By this time, I was trembling as he gave us the information we needed to hear. To our great surprise two little spots were found—one on each breast. One spot was 4 mm long and the other 2 mm, thus tiny at this time. Nevertheless, I was upset that there was anything at all. Then Dr Bayly examined my breasts carefully and could not find any lumps, thank goodness! The radiologist advised me to have another mammogram in one year's time. Dr Bayly advised me to take some deep breaths and listen carefully while he gave me additional information. He began by saying that older women like me (I'm 72) develop cysts in their breasts and that's all it might be. I could see that my husband was quite relieved to hear that. Not me! I have to get used to the idea that 2 little spots were discovered in my breasts—they are there! I cannot stop thinking about that fact, and it is a true as Dr Bayly showed us their location.

Alex took me out for lunch in an effort to get me to relax and it worked somewhat. After a blood test, we arrived home and I knew my 3 daughters needed to know this. I had to try to rest before calling Jacquie, Michelle and Allison. I called my two sisters Liesje and Lillian as well. Naturally they were surprised as no sisters, aunts, grandmothers, or female cousins have had breast cancer as far as we knew. I called my aunt in Holland to make sure and she affirmed that it was so. She asked me to let her know. I promised her I would if indeed those tiny spots were cancer or not. Therefore, I am a woman who has not inherited this disease at all. I knew that the possibility existed anyway but since all my previous mammograms had been fine this news was a huge shock. I had never thought or really worried about that possibility at all.

I met Dr. Joseph (my psychiatrist) the following week and he advised me definitely to inform my granddaughters Emily and Rachel this weekend. He agreed that one year was too long to wait for another mammogram to see whether those little spots show any change and 6 months is a better idea. I called Dr. Bayly and his assistant informed me that the radiologist's suggestion would be followed. This news left me astonished but that's the way it was. So, now I will try to continue living my life for another year and see what the results of my next mammogram will be. Thankfully after several years, there has been no change and I am able to enjoy my life.

Carnegie Hall — newchoir — Toronto's rock choir

YES, IT'S TRUE, my eldest daughter, Jacquie, stood on the stage in that world-renowned venue to sing, in March 2015, and her parents were there to bask in reflective glory.

Jacquie belongs to a co-ed choir in Toronto called newchoir consisting of 150 members. She loves it! She sings tenor. The choir was invited to come to New York City to perform there. Excitedly, she called us and asked if we would like to go to New York City too. We answered with an enthusiastic YES! We hadn't been to that amazing city for many years so we jumped at the chance to go again.

They all marched onto the stage in perfect order as they had practised a number of times, it was seamless! We were so excited! As our daughter looked at the packed house, she told us later that it meant a lot to her to know that her parents were there to share this experience with her. Jacquie is 50 years old. Lovely to know how much she appreciated us being there. The performance was phenomenal! Jacquie has red hair so it was easy to find her in that large choir. The audience roared its' enthusiastic approval for such a musical treat to hear chorale music in that beautiful setting. We clapped and sang along to the Lions Sleeps Tonight as invited to by noted Musical Director, Deke Sharon of Pitch Perfect movie fame. All the months of hard work by newchoir was worth it to hear them sing a cappella in that storied venue.

newchoir on stage at Carnegie Hall

FAMILY REUNIONS

WHAT IS MORE exciting than looking forward to a family reunion? Every 2 years my family of origin, the de Burger Family, has a family reunion. This tradition began in 2009, two years after the death of my father in 2007. Adults and children converge on a resort in Barrie in June and joyfully greet all family members as they arrive. Some come on Friday, some on Saturday morning. The family now spans four generations. We have 8 children under age 10 and they play together as though they had seen each other last week. Such a delight to watch! There is no whining, fighting nor is anyone excluded. Their play never needs to be organised as they decide themselves whether to just run, play on the playground equipment, whatever comes to mind and all join in happily.

The resort also has a pool which we all appreciate. There are plenty of activities for all. We, de Burger siblings, are the senior members of the family. Erna, Ron, Frank, Liesje and Lillian and our spouses cheerfully catch up on family news. It's always such a marvellous time for us to be together as we live in various parts of the province. Even so, we are close. It's wonderful to watch all the cousins interact and enjoy each other's company. Some of our nieces and nephews are musical and bring their guitars for our enjoyment. Even the little ones are learning to play. Peals of laughter can be heard frequently as well as singing by some who love to do that.

It happens that some cannot attend every time due to other commitments. They are missed but not forgotten. But the reunions are the glue that hold our family together.

The food for the weekend is pot luck, we all bring various dishes and there is always more than enough for all. Everyone brings their own drinks and snacks for their family.

Family Reunion picture 2016

de Burgers with Spouses

Ron (1942-2016)

IT'S DIFFICULT TO believe and understand that my brother Ron is gone. I miss him so much! Ron was just 14 months younger than me. On Friday August 5, 2016 his life's journey came to a peaceful end. He died in his sleep at home. He had told me years ago that he hoped he would pass this way. God was merciful and granted his wish. Ron would have been 74 years old just two weeks later on August 27.

Ron was diagnosed with aggressive leukemia and was determined to beat it. Many times he declared, "I'm not going anywhere!" That strong Dutch stubbornness evidenced itself throughout all the miserable chemo treatments that he endured, always remaining positive and so grateful for our visits and love. He fought this terrible disease for two years with every ounce of strength he had. His wife Fran was at his side throughout this awful journey. Theirs was a genuine love story. Ron and Fran had celebrated their 50th wedding anniversary on May 14 of 2016, just 3 months before his death. David and Paul and their wives were incredible in the constant support they gave their parents in every way possible. He loved his family deeply and was elated at the birth of his only grandson Ryan, son of David and Michelle.

In June 2016, we had enjoyed our biennial de Burger Family Reunion at Carriage Hills Resort in Muskoka. It was the best turnout ever with 30 family members present. Ron and Fran's family were all there and Friday night was a siblings' reunion before all the nieces and nephews and their children arrived on

Saturday. As such it was an evening of reminiscing and laughter although Ron seemed somewhat pensive. After breakfast he gathered the five of us together and told us, "My cancer is back." What a shock! I had not expected that at all. In typical Ron fashion he asked us not to tell our family members as he wanted everyone to enjoy the weekend as we always had, without his leukemia being the focus. On Saturday, my 75th birthday was celebrated with a lovely cake and Ron and Fran's little grandson Ryan helped me to blow out the candles. In the pictures Ryan was right there close to the cake ready to help me. No, there were not 75 of them! Even between the two of us I don't think we could have extinguished that many. Ron and Fran were close by as well not wanting to miss anything with their only grandchild. Paul and Angela, Ryan's godparents, are also in the picture. On Sunday afternoon before everyone left to return to their homes, we gathered for a group picture as we always do. Unfortunately, Ron stood at the very back as he always did, where it is difficult to see him.

Just 7 weeks later, my sister Lillian called to tell me that our beloved Ron had died during the night—August 5. I'm glad that Alex was home as I sobbed uncontrollably in disbelief. We had just seen him, joked with him, discussed family events. How could he be gone so quickly?

Fran had checked on Ron before she went to bed around 11 pm and he was sleeping normally. For some unknown reason she got up around 3 am and checked on him again and to her shock, he had died. She called Paul and Angela immediately who lived in Oakville just 30 minutes away from Waterdown. As soon as they got there Paul took over, called 9-1-1, and he and Angela consoled Fran and each other. I know it must have been terrible for all of them. They called David and Michelle in Guelph who were also in disbelief.

When the family called the oncologist to report that Ron had passed away, even he was surprised as death had not seemed imminent to him.

Ron was our mentor. He was our father's executor and kept all of us informed of information we needed to know. Ron was extremely knowledgeable about many things due to his numerous varied interests. He read several newspapers every day. Watching sports on television was his diversion and relaxation. He loved the Blue

Jays, the Ottawa Senators and tennis. His hugs and sense of humour endeared him to all of us. He was popular with his colleagues wherever he worked. He had important positions in three provinces in the field of Public Health in which he was considered an expert. I was very proud of him always.

As I was writing my memoirs, I would always send them to Ron by email to ask if I had forgotten something, was wrong in some aspect and he would often add to my efforts. Men and women have different memories of the same event and so his feedback was invaluable to me and I appreciated it. He and I were the only ones who remembered the journey to Canada by ship, those first very difficult years in Canada, our living conditions in Warren, St. Charles, in the bush and in Dogpatch (Rockville), the family tragedies of losing Marianne and Willy, Dad's heart attack underground, we remembered best as we were the two oldest of 7 children.

I will love, miss and remember my brother Ron for the rest of my life. Rest in Peace, my dear brother Ron. You have earned your rest.

HOCKEY EFFECTS

HE SHOOTS, HE scores! Ever since the fifties, hockey has impacted my life in various ways. My father and three brothers were all huge sports fans of many different sports. It was inevitable that I be drawn in as well as some point. I'm not sure how or when it happened but meeting my husband Alex Fex in 1959 accelerated that interest without a doubt. When we met at Pine Cove Lodge on the French River in August of that year, I had no way of knowing what a superb athlete he was!!

My Dad and my brothers began to watch and enjoy hockey on television on Saturday nights and very often Alex would join them at our home in Rockville aka Dogpatch, near Creighton Mine. Of course, I wanted to be there too! Dad bought a mechanical table hockey game which all the men played frequently with lots of yelling and fun. Just after my brother Willy was killed in 1960, it was an excellent diversion for my brothers and my boyfriend in those early difficult months.

During that winter I started to attend high school hockey games as Alex played for Sudbury High School and I attended Copper Cliff High which had a strong rivalry with High School. Alex was an excellent player always playing with great energy. Sometimes, he got over-excited which resulted in penalties of course. He attempted to hold himself in check somewhat until near the end of the game. That way, he explained to me, he wouldn't miss playing too much of the game by being penalized. Several times, the next day I would be greeted by some of the Copper Cliff players asking me to keep him in check, as if I had any control over what happened on the ice. I would tell him on the phone that night and he would laugh and tell me to just forget about it. I developed a love for hockey during my high school years.

When Alex attended Ryerson Institute of Technology, now called Ryerson University, he easily achieved a place on the varsity team there. Again, he excelled and in fact that entire team was a powerhouse and won the Intercollegiate Championship in 1962. No Ryerson Rams hockey team has been able to do that since then.

In 2012, the team was inducted into the Ryerson Sports Hall of Fame. I was there in Toronto accompanied by a number of family members, even grandchildren. That was a truly wonderful day for all of us and we were justifiably proud. The current coach of the team told their story and pointed out that the "silver foxes" should be an example to them to encourage them to strive for the same result. Every year since then the team members have been invited back to Ryerson to play against the current hockey team. Sadly, there are fewer players able to come every year as age is having its' effects.

The university has treated these alumnae royally ever since. Team member Don Desjardins purchased seats for each team member and there's a plaque with their name on their seat. Our grandkids love to find their Grandpa's seat and sit in it whenever they are at the Ryerson Arena, now called the Mattamy Athletic Centre.

Oldtimer Hockey took over our lives when Alex turned 35 and the Walden Oldtimers Hockey Team was formed. He is the only member of that founding team who is still actively playing hockey. He plays three times a week at Walden Arena in Lively. At his age of nearly 78 that is remarkable. He loves it!

In 2010, Vancouver hosted the Winter Olympics to all of Canada's joy. I'm an avid Olympics fan enjoying watching many different sports, my favourite being Figure Skating. Canada won gold due to the perfection of the dance pair Virtue and Moir. The entire Olympics lasted a full 17 days. Naturally, we watched the men and women's hockey teams as well. The women's team won a gold medal on Day 14 of the Olympics beating the US team. Now it was up to the men to replicate that feat. When the men's team hit the ice, the fans gave them a raucous reception to encourage them. They were playing arch rivals USA. At the end of regulation time the score was tied. Just seconds into overtime, Canada's best hockey player, Sidney Crosby, scored! Pandemonium everywhere across Canada where people had gathered to watch. Gold Medal there too.

Hockey will be a part of our lives forever! Whenever we are in Toronto, we try to go to watch our talented grandsons, Matthieu and Nicholas play. Our older grandson Trent played too when he was younger, as did his sister Rachel. Our sons-in-law Scott and Rey are playing oldtimer hockey now and often ask Alex to play with them. He loves that! Our youngest daughter Allison has recently taken up the sport. We have attended our great grandson Aayden's games in the Sudbury area. That was fun! He was always very happy to see that we were there.

The effects of Canada's national sport, hockey, have permeated our lives nearly all of our lives. It has been a uniting factor for this family and this country.

Alex at Mattamy Arena (2019)

Matriarch

I bet you didn't think I'd own up to it, but here it is. I am a matriarch. The term sounds old, doesn't it? But that is me! I am female and the oldest of all the de Burgers alive today whether they live in The Netherlands or Canada. I attained this title after my father, Florent de Burger, died in 2007 at the age of 91. I did not grasp it until sometime later and the realisation came as a shock, let me tell you! Whoever expects to become a matriarch? It was never a goal of mine! Mind you, I'm glad that I'm here to appreciate it.

Since it is my reality now, I regard it as an honour. It's the first time I've had this title so I plan to thoroughly enjoy it! Let's see now, what does a matriarch do? I'm at the top of the ladder of life. Hopefully someone is holding this ladder at the bottom in case it wobbles. I don't want to fall! No, thank you!

Being the head of four generations will not be experienced by many of my contemporaries. My three wonderful daughters and their spouses make me very proud. My numerous nieces and nephews are all great productive people. Of course, I have the five most incredible grandchildren in the world. Oh, and my great grandson melts my heart simply with his smile and his, "Hi Oma". When we went to watch him play soccer recently, he spotted us immediately. He told me and his Opa that he said to himself in his head that he would come to hug us when the coach allowed him leave to the pitch for a bit. Smiling, he came running at us with both his arms wide open ready for a big hug.

Looking back over my life from my childhood to becoming a great grandmother, I have so many things for which to be grateful. My marriage of over fifty years to Alex, the love of my life is the most important facet of my life. My foundation was provided by my parents, who taught me the importance of family values and hard work by modelling it for me. Their decision in 1951 to immigrate to Canada seeking a better life for their family was of course a major life - changing event for me and my siblings. Family always came first and so it is for me. I appreciate my always supportive siblings to whom I feel close no matter where they live. My faith has assisted me through difficult hurdles enabling me to reach this wonderful stage of my life. I've had the good fortune of having wonderful loyal friends for many years. Being a matriarch is good!

My Life So Far - Changes

AT MY PRESENT age, I decided to look back at my life experiences and lifestyles. I knew there had been many changes and examining those is what I need to do. I am not ill, thank goodness. In fact, I am fortunate to have good health.

Having been born in The Netherlands in 1941 resulted in my young childhood being very stable, totally loved by my parents, numerous aunts, uncles, cousins and most importantly, my grandparents and my Great Grandmother. I visited them all often and knew I was deeply loved and very happy.

When my parents made the wrenching decision to leave our homeland to immigrate to Canada, my childhood changed drastically. I missed my grandparents and all the extended family dreadfully. We were all alone in this new country where we didn't speak the language, understand the culture, and the unforeseen shocking climate. That first winter in 1951 brought huge amounts of snow and bitter cold. I was not used to this and did not have proper clothing to cope with this weather. School was also very different. Attending a one-room school with both boys and girls was surprising. In Holland I had attended a girls' school to which I walked. Here, the teacher's father picked me up in his truck and drove us to school every morning. Learning English was exciting for this 10 year- old.

I had to assume many chores which was new to me. In Holland my mother's sisters or our housekeeper had done all of this. Mom was sick at times and Dad was at work all day. As the eldest and a girl, I learned to peel potatoes, help with laundry, clean the house and take care of younger siblings if that was needed. The fact that our family had to share a three-bedroom house with another family of six was difficult for all of us especially Mom.

My family moved three times within that first year which was a constant change of homes and schools. I didn't like that. On my 11th birthday a baby sister was born while we were living in St. Charles where I learned functional French very quickly. I loved her dearly but had no idea just how ill and handicapped she was.

Living in the bush behind Creighton was another huge challenge. There were no neighbours, no friends. No electricity or water. My baby sister died while we were living there and soon after her death, Mom gave birth to a beautiful healthy baby girl. Attending Creighton Mine Public School gave me the opportunity to begin to make friends in this new country. The constant love of my parents helped me to accept all the transitions in my life.

After one year, we happily moved from the bush into a small friendly community referred to as Dogpatch where I made my first best friend in Canada. Her name was Lorraine Mead and even though she has died recently I will never forget her. Another close family death in March of 1960, my healthy 15-year old brother Willy, was devastating.

As an adult, I achieved my teaching certificate at North Bay Teachers' College in 1962, and began my teaching career at Creighton Mine Public School. I loved every day that I taught. I had really found my niche in society and life.

In 1963, I married Alex, my high school sweetheart. We lived in Creighton Mine for nine years and two daughters were born while we lived there. Becoming a mother was unbelievably joyful. The wonderful neighbours made living there so amiable and fun. Everyone looked out for each others' children.

I returned to teaching when my little girls were older and was hired in 1970 to teach Grade 2 at Our Lady of Fatima School. The large congenial staff was close to the same age and we developed deep friendships and enjoyed many wonderful social activities which included our spouses. Those were happy and fulfilling years for me. In 1974, I gave birth to my third healthy baby girl. Our family was complete. We were contented home owners by now, again in a wonderful neighbourhood where we gained life-long friends. I was singing in the church choir beginning then and have continued to do so until today.

Living on Moxam Drive for 33 years gave me the opportunity to develop my love of gardening and provided me with a room of my own where I happily installed and filled bookshelves. I love reading and here I was able to store many well-loved volumes to peruse often. It was a wonderful neighbourhood to raise our children. There was a huge yard where they could play with their friends and the spacious house allowed for entertaining family and friends both for our daughters and us.

My husband entered politics in 1976, which really caused our lives to adapt in many ways. I was extremely busy being a wife, mother, teacher and taking university courses as well in the evenings. Community involvement, children's activities, increased social life led to some overwhelming times for me.

Our first grandchild was born in 1988. I could never have imagined the actual infusion of love I experienced the first time I held this beautiful baby girl in my arms. Four more delightful grandchildren followed to enhance my life. They are so much fun!!

I retired in 1996 and cared for my mother during her terminal illness. She died in 1997 which left a huge void in my life. I visited my father often afterwards as he was very lonely, though thankfully, he lived another 10 years until 2007.

I became a great grandmother in 2009. My granddaughter had a baby—almost difficult to absorb. When I held him in my arms the truth of this marvellous event was real. He has brought me so much joy and love that I feel blessed to know this special little boy.

Now in my late 70's, we are living in a spacious apartment in the largest apartment building in Sudbury. I serve on the Board of the Rockview Towers Older Adult Club. The reception we received after we moved here was so friendly and warm. We have made many new friends and know many acquaintances, as well. There are so many social events happening here that we are enjoying our lives immensely. My husband also does a great deal of volunteer work helping in the garden area. I have developed many new routines as living in each new home has required. The community is also most supportive in sad times or illness.

At this point in my life I understand that by volunteering and being open to new friendships I have enjoyed a good life. I am healthy, as is my husband and we are happy together. We still really like each other - after 57 years of marriage!

CPSIA information can be obtained
at www.ICGtesting.com
Printed in the USA
BVHW022334230521
607936BV00001B/1

9 781525 577420